The Eugenic Marriage

Volume II

by

W. Grant Hague

ISBN: 978-1-63923-214-7

Printed: May 2022

Cover Art By: Amit Paul

Published and Distributed By:
Lushena Books
607 Country Club Drive, Unit E
Bensenville, IL 60106
www.lushenabooksinc.com/books

ISBN: 978-1-63923-214-7

The Eugenic Marriage

A Personal Guide to the New Science of Better Living and Better Babies

By W. GRANT HAGUE, M. D.

College of Physicians and Surgeons (Columbia University), New York; Member of County Medical Society, and of the American Medical Association

In Four Volumes

VOLUME II

New York

THE REVIEW OF REVIEWS COMPANY

1914

TABLE OF CONTENTS

CHAPTER XIV

A MOTHER'S DUTY TO HER DAUGHTER

What a mother should tell her little girl—Where do babies come from—How baby birds and fish come from eggs—How other animals have little nests of their own—The duty of mothers to instruct and direct—What a mother should tell her daughter—Every mother should[Pg iv] regard this duty as sacred—Every female child is a possible future mother—Motherhood the highest function of the sex—Health the one necessary essential —Symptoms of the first, or beginning menstruation—The period of puberty in the female—Changes in the reproductive organs at puberty—The female generative organs—The function of the reproductive organs—The age of puberty in the female— The function of the ovary—The function of the womb—Why menstruation occurs every twenty-eight days—The male or papa egg—The function of the spermatozoa—"Tell the whole story"—"How do these spermatozoa get there"—The union of the species—"How can a baby live in there for such a long time"—How the baby gets its nourishment in the womb—Girls must not become mothers

CHAPTER XV

PREPARING FOR MOTHERHOOD

Menstruation—Irregular menstruation—Changes in the quantity of the flow—How the womb is held in place—Symptoms of menstruation—Menstruation should not be accompanied with pain—Don't give your daughters patent medicines, or "Female Regulators"—Take your daughter to the doctor—Leucorrhea in girls—Bathing when menstruating—Constipation and displaced wombs—Dress and menstruation—Absence of menstruation, or amenorrhea—Treatment of amenorrhea—Painful menstruation, or dysmenorrhea—Causes of dysmenorrhea—Treatment of dysmenorrhea—Sterility in the female—Conditions which affect the fertility of women—Climate, station in life, season of the year, age, the tendency to miscarry—Causes of sterility in the female—Displacement of womb—Diseases of womb, ovaries, or tubes—Malformations—Lacerations—Tumors— Leucorrhea— Physical debility—Obesity—Special poisons—"Knack of miscarrying"—Miscarriage—Cause of miscarriage—The course

The Baby

CHAPTER XVI

HYGIENE AND DEVELOPMENT OF THE BABY

CHAPTER XVII

BABY'S FEEDING HABITS

CHAPTER XVIII

BABY'S GOOD AND BAD HABITS—FOOD FORMULAS

Artificial Feeding

CHAPTER XIX

ARTIFICIAL FEEDING

CHAPTER XX

ARTIFICIAL FEEDING (*continued*)

during the second year—Sample meals for a child three years of age—The diet of older children—Meats, vegetables, cereals, bread, desserts, fruits

What Mothers Should Know

CHAPTER XXI

THE EDUCATION OF THE MOTHER

What mothers should know about the care of children during illness—A sick child should be in bed—The diet of the sick child—A child is the most helpless living thing—The delicate child—How to feed the delicate child—How to bathe the delicate child—Airing the delicate child—Habits of the delicate child—Indiscriminate feeding—Poor appetite—Loss of appetite —Treatment of loss of appetite—Overeating in infancy—What correct eating means—Bran as a food—Breakfast for a child at school—Lunch for a child at school—Bran muffins for school children—Bran muffins in constipation—Hysterical children— What a mother should know about cathartics and[Pg vii] how to give a dose of castor oil—Castor oil—Calomel—Citrate of Magnesium—When to use castor oil—When to use calomel— Vaccination—Time for vaccination—Methods of vaccination— Symptoms of successful vaccination

CHAPTER XXII

CONSTIPATION IN INFANTS AND CHILDREN

Constipation—Regularity of bowel function—The function of the stomach—Fermentation—Incomplete constipation— Importance of a clean bowel—A daily movement of the bowel necessary—Constipation in breast-fed infants—Treatment of constipation in breast-fed infants—Constipation in bottle-fed infants—Treatment of constipation in bottle-fed infants— Constipation in children over two years of age—Diet list for constipation in children—Bran muffins in constipation— Treatment of obstinate constipation—Oil injections in constipation

CHAPTER XXIII

CONSTIPATION IN WOMEN

Chief cause of constipation in women—Constipation a cause of domestic unhappiness—The requirements of good health—The cost of constipation—Constipation and social exigencies—One of the important duties of mothers—Constipation and diseases of women—Constipation is always harmful—Constipation and pregnancy—Explanation of incomplete constipation—Causes of constipation—Negligence—Lack of exercise—Lack of water—Lack of bulk in the food taken—Abuse of cathartic drugs and aperient waters—Overeating—Treatment of constipation in women

SEX HYGIENE FOR THE BOY

CHAPTER XII

"The evil that men do lives after them. The good is often interred with them."

"The pleasure in living is to meet temptation and not yield to it." Elmer Lee, M. D.

BUILDING OUR BOYS

A Word to Parents—Interest in Sex Hygiene—The "Social Evil"—Ten Millions Suffering with Venereal Diseases in the United States—Immorality not Confined to Large Cities—Venereal Diseases Common in Country Places—What Are the Consequences of Venereal Disease to the Boy?—Gonorrhea, or Clap—Symptoms of Gonorrhea in the Male—Complications of Gonorrhea—Syphilis, or the "Pox"—How Syphilis is Acquired—Syphilis Attacks Every Organ in the Body—Not Possible to Tell When Cured—The Chancre—Systematic or Constitutional Symptoms—Mucous Patches and Ulcers—Syphilis of the Blood Vessels and Lymphatic Glands—The Interior Organs—Brain and Spinal Cord—The Nose, Eye, Ear, Throat—Hair and Nails—What the Boy with Venereal Disease

May Cause in Others—The Infected Wife—A Girl's Fate When She Marries—Young Wife Rendered Sterile—Young Wife Made to Miscarry—Is the Husband to Blame?—Building the Man—Age of Puberty—"Internal Secretion."

A Word to Parents.—Within recent times the subject of sex hygiene has been freely discussed by members of the medical profession and through them the general public has been made more or less acquainted with the problem. It has therefore acquired a degree of genuine interest which speaks well for the future of the eugenic ideal. Eugenics is based to a very large extent upon the principles underlying sex hygiene.

As a result of this widespread interest and investigation, we have discovered that the only method that promises actual progress, is to talk plainly and to tell the actual truth. The day of the prude has passed. To attempt to achieve results in the education of youth in[Pg 140] sex problems, without giving, facts, is wasted effort. To give facts we must explain each problem so that its principles may be clearly understood and its meaning grasped. To point out the duty of youth is not sufficient. They must be shown why it is to their best interest to live the clean life. In every department of education we are beginning to appreciate that to achieve results it must be based upon the individual equation. This is why we have found it necessary to assert that it is the duty of parents to make sex hygiene a personal matter and to acquaint their children with the facts relating to this problem. It has been discovered, however, that a very large percentage of parents are inadequately informed on these subjects, in fact they know practically nothing about the actual facts which they are supposed to teach. I shall try to tell the story in a way which every parent will understand.

When a boy reaches the age of puberty he is susceptible to sexual desire. If he has not been told the story of his growth from boyhood to man's estate he will either begin to abuse himself, or he will be later enticed to commit himself to intercourse with some unclean female and he will acquire a disease as a result.

Inasmuch as it has been asserted that practically every boy has been addicted to self-abuse at some time, and that eighty per cent. of all males, between the ages of sixteen and thirty years, are victims of venereal disease, it would seem justifiable to assume that the boys who are informed of the facts in time are the boys who constitute the percentage who escape. This, of course, may not be literally true, but it is a reasonable assumption.

While self-abuse is a pernicious habit and may be attended with serious consequences, it is not a disease and, as will be explained later, it can be cured. It is therefore a menace to the individual, not to the race, and consequently need not concern us at the present time. On the other hand the venereal diseases are not to be considered as individual problems since they affect the welfare of the race. The venereal diseases which we will consider are gonorrhea and syphilis.

The Social Evil.—It has been estimated that there are[Pg 141] more than *ten millions* of people in this country to-day suffering from the effects of venereal diseases. In New York city alone, there are *two million* victims suffering from the direct or indirect consequences of these diseases. It has been authoritatively asserted that, out of every ten men between the ages of sixteen and thirty, eight have, or have had, one or other of these diseases. When it is remembered that these diseases are not merely temporary incidents, but that they may be regarded as practically incurable in the vast majority, because of antagonistic social conditions and ignorance, and that they are highly infectious, we may begin to realize how important they are from the standpoint of race regeneration.

Statistics of these conditions are never reliable because much of the evil is hidden and lied about. It is quite probable,—if the estimates were based upon absolute knowledge—that the extent of the prevalency of these diseases would be greatly increased rather than reduced. It is however a fact, that the combined ravages of the Great White Plague, leprosy, yellow fever, and small-pox, are merely incidents compared to the effects which the venereal diseases have had upon mankind. It is useless to think that these diseases can be driven out of the land. Any hope of this nature is the impression of the dreamer. By a propaganda of education, by the spread of the eugenic idea and ideal, we may, however, reasonably hope to minimize the evil and, at least, to protect the innocent.

The Sources of Immorality.—It is a fallacious idea to assume that the sources of immorality are confined to the large cities. This is far from the truth. In smaller towns and country places the diseases are quite common and conditions there tend to the spread of the contagion in a more intimate and a more harmful way. The individuals who are most likely to become affected are those most liable to succumb to temptation and whose home ties are of the best. There are many instances on record where one or two loose women spread the infection all over the country communities, infecting boys and men alike. No one can estimate what the final effect of such an epidemic may mean or how many innocent[Pg 142] individuals may have their lives wrecked as a direct consequence. It is because these consequences are the product of ignorance in a very large percentage of the cases that there is such urgent need for enlightenment. It is at least our plain duty to tell the boy the actual facts—to post him with reference to consequences. The more thoroughly we instruct him in the elementary facts relative to the venereal diseases, the safer he will be from temptation, and if he possesses this knowledge and acquires disease, he will be more likely to immediately seek competent aid and advice.

WHAT ARE THE CONSEQUENCES OF VENEREAL DISEASE TO THE BOY HIMSELF?

Gonorrhea or "Clap."—This is the most frequent of the venereal diseases. It is also the most serious. It is an unfortunate fact, that in the past,—and even to-day—boys have been told that gonorrhea is no worse than "a bad cold." This lie has been responsible for much evil and a great amount of unnecessary suffering and misery.

Gonorrhea is caused by a germ, obtained, as a rule, during intercourse with an infected person. This germ is called gonococcus. It thrives on any mucous membrane; it is not, therefore, limited to the sexual organs. For this reason it may attack any part of the body where mucous membrane is. It is particularly liable to damage, sometimes seriously and permanently, the eye. It may be spread from one person to another, or from any infected article to a person in numerous ways. The innocent may thus suffer as a result of the carelessness of the vicious.

The Symptoms of Gonorrhea in the Male are slight itching and burning of the mouth of the urethra. This is noticeable at any time from the third to the fourteenth day after exposure. These symptoms become more pronounced and a slight discharge appears. The patient is compelled to urinate frequently and it is painful and difficult. The discharge increases, it becomes thicker and looks like ordinary yellow pus. If the case is a severe one, the discharge may be blood stained, and[Pg 143] if this symptom is present urination is more painful and more frequent.

In about ten days the disease reaches its height; it remains stationary for a number of weeks and then slowly, seemingly, gets better. The discharge grows thinner, less in quantity and lighter in color. It may refuse, despite the most careful and efficient treatment, to stop altogether; it is then known as "gleet." If the discharge stops completely the patient is apparently cured, as far as any external manifestation of the disease is concerned. *In seventy-five per cent. of the cases, however, this apparent cure is no cure at all, as will be seen later.*

Certain complications are likely to arise in the course of gonorrhea. The infection itself may be of such an acute or virulent type, that it invades the deeper structures of its own accord and despite the most careful, competent treatment; or if the treatment is not adequate or skillful it may be forced backward; or through neglect in not beginning the right kind of treatment in times, a simple infection may grow in degree into a serious disease, and invade the more important structures. In this way are produced disease of the bladder, prostate gland, seminal vesicles, testicles, and of the kidneys. Gonorrheal rheumatism may follow, and even disease of the lining membrane of the heart, and death.

When disease of the deeper parts occur the patient is frequently incapacitated and compelled to go to bed. He may have chills, fever and sweats, intense pain and the passage of bloody urine. He may have to be operated upon, and his general health may be permanently wrecked. So long as the germs are present there is danger despite the most scientific treatment. It is not the quality of the treatment that is at fault, it is the presence of the germs; and since it is impossible to pursue any certain method of eradication, we must continue treatment—as long as the germs are present—and hope for favorable results. The infection may last for many years. The germs having found entrance into the small tubes in the interior organs they can only be dislodged with difficulty, if at all. These pockets of germs may be excited[Pg 144] to renewed activity by sexual intercourse, or by injury to the parts, and may reinfect the patient at any times. In a very considerable number of these cases where the deeper structures are involved, the patient may recover from the acute or painful period of the disease, only to find that he is sterile. There are many such cases, and the most vindictive individual who may believe that every who sins should be punished will admit that sterility, as the price of a moment's forgetfulness, is a terrible fee to pay.

Syphilis, or the "Pox," is an infectious, germ blood disease. It is most frequently acquired through sexual intercourse.

It may be acquired by direct contact with a diseased person. In order to render such contact effective, it is essential that the skin of the healthy person be abraded, or the contact may be directly on a mucous membrane, as the mouth in the act of kissing.

It may be acquired by using any article which has been used by a syphilitic, as a drinking cup, or towel.

It may be acquired through hereditary transmission.

Surgeons frequently contract syphilis while operating on, or examining patients who have the disease. Dentists may convey it by means of instruments which have not been rendered aseptic, or thoroughly clean. Using a towel which has been used by a syphilitic has many times conveyed the infection to an innocent party. For this reason the roller towel has been done away with, and some states have legislated against its use in hotels and other public places. To use dishes, spoons, tobacco pipe, beer glasses, etc., which have been used by one having the disease is an absolutely certain way of being infected. Cigars which may have been made by a syphilitic will infect whoever smokes them with the virus of the disease. Syphilis has been known to have been caught from using the church communion cup. The public drinking-cup has been a prolific source of syphilitic dissemination to innocents. Legislators are just waking up to the danger that lurks in this institution and it will no doubt be done away with, not only in public places, but on all railroad and steamboat lines.[Pg 145]

An infected mother can transmit syphilis to her child. If the father is affected, but not the wife, the child may escape.

Syphilis attacks every organ in the human body. The actual degree of infection has no relation to the size or character of the external manifestations. The external evidence may be minute and insignificant, while the internal extent and ravages of the disease may be tremendous and of large proportions. Many men when asked regarding incidents of the long ago, may state, "Oh, yes, I had a chancre twenty-five years ago, but it was a very small affair and soon healed up and was cured." Yet that same little chancre, that made only a mild impression on the man's mind, may, and most probably will, be the direct cause of that man's death.

It is not possible to tell with absolute certainty that an individual is suffering with syphilis by any known test. The most recent one—the Wassermann test—is not absolute by any means.

The first symptoms, or what is known as the initial lesion of syphilis, is the chancre.

The Chancre is a small, hard tumor, or it may be a small ulcer with a hard base, or it may simply appear as a thin small patch on any mucous membrane. It is not painful, it can be moved if taken between the fingers, showing it is not attached to the deep structures, and when it is so moved it is not tender or sore. Any little lump which ulcerates located on the genitals must be regarded with suspicion. Boys and men should not be satisfied with any offhand statement that, "it is nothing." It may be a chancre, and it may be exceedingly serious if not properly diagnosed.

Systemic, or constitutional symptoms, begin to show themselves any time from the sixth to the tenth week after the appearance of the chancre.

Eruptions of the Skin characterize every case of syphilis. They occur in all degrees from the mild rash to the foul ulcer. The ulcerative process is very often extensive and loathsome.

Mucous Patches and Ulcers affect the mucous membranes. The mouth and throat are favorite locations[Pg 146] for these lesions. They occur in the anus and rectum, and may be mistaken in that region for other serious conditions. Men who drink and smoke suffer as a rule severely from mucous patches in the mouth and throat.

Syphilis attacks the blood vessels and the lymphatic glands. These cases may have been unrecognized, and may have existed for many years. A man may die from a rupture of a blood vessel in the brain during middle life as a consequence of a forgotten, supposedly cured case of syphilis many years before.

The Interior Organs may be attacked by syphilis. As a result we get disease of the liver, heart, stomach, kidneys, lungs, and other parts. It has been suggested that many diseases affecting these organs, for which treatment proves unsatisfactory, may have had their origin in a former syphilis.

The Brain and Spinal Cord are quite often the seat of syphilitic affections. A tumor, known by the name of "gumma," is the result. The blood vessels of the entire nervous system may be affected and, as a consequence, we often see cases of paralysis, apoplexy, epilepsy, locomotor ataxia and death.

The Nose, Eye, Ear, Throat, are frequently very seriously compromised as a result of the syphilitic poison. Deformity, caused by rotting of the bones of these parts is not infrequent. Loss of voice, or smell, or hearing, or sight, may result.

The Hair and Nails may fall out. The bones may ulcerate and rot. The organs of procreation usually participate in the degenerative process. Virility is destroyed, and impotence is quite common after a severe attack.

WHAT THE BOY WITH VENEREAL DISEASE MAY CAUSE IN OTHERS

Gonorrhea.—When the average boy acquires gonorrhea he frequently does not know, for many weeks, that he is the victim of a dangerous, infectious disease. He appreciates probably, that it relates to the sexual indiscretion[Pg 147] he was guilty of, and feels that it is something to be ashamed of. He therefore hides his condition, confides in no one, and blindly hopes it will get better somehow or at some time. Meantime the disease, which may have been mild at the beginning, is gradually gaining ground and strength, and his neglect may eventuate in lifelong misery. No means are taken to guard against spreading the infection, the discharge may lodge on his fingers and he may infect his eyes and may lose his sight because he did not know that the discharge is one of the most dangerous fluids known. It may get on water-closet seats and infect others. Eventually he is compelled to seek aid, and he may, after a long period, be freed from the immediate consequences of his folly. At a later date he marries, and as previously explained, he infects his wife. This is the beginning of much of the domestic infelicity that is so prevalent to-day, and, inasmuch as it is a subject that should be thoroughly understood by every woman and mother, I shall carefully and clearly explain its significance and its consequences.

Let us first, however, briefly consider what may occur to others if the boy is unfortunate enough to acquire syphilis. Again the boy fails to comprehend the nature of his affliction. There is imminent danger of the members of his household becoming infected. He uses the same dishes, spoons, towels, and utensils, any one of which may convey the disease to his father, mother, sister, or brother. He may use the common drinking glass in school, college, or office, and spread the disease in this way. He may kiss any member of his family, or a baby, and infect them. He may have his hair cut, or be shaved, and the virus may be spread around in this way if the barber does not sterilize the article used,—which he never does. He may drink at a soda fountain, or at a saloon, and the next individual to use the same glass may acquire the disease. He is a menace to the individual, to the community, and to the race. Wives often acquire syphilis from their husbands.

The Infected Wife.—It has been previously stated that eight out of every ten males between the ages of sixteen and thirty, have had or have, gonorrhea or syphilis.[Pg 148] Seventy-five per cent. of these cases have not been cured. About thirty-five per cent. of these are destined to infect wife, or wife and children, and in all probability many others.

If a young wife acquires infection from her husband, she is exactly in the same condition as the diseased boy,—she does not know what ails her, so she wastes precious time in unprofitable worry. Why should she know what the trouble is? She came to the marriage bed pure, and clean, and healthy. Her previous education did not include instruction which would even help her to guess what the trouble might be. She is simply conscious of new distressing conditions which she does not understand. She may try to believe that these conditions are incidental to the change in her life. Shortly, however, the discharge, which she has had for a number of weeks, and which she thought was only a leucorrhea, or "the whites," becomes so profuse and nasty that she begins douching. This procedure simply blinds her to the true nature of the affection, and in the end she is driven, ashamed and reluctant, to consult a physician. She may be informed that her condition is bad, and that it will be necessary that she submit to a course of treatment. After a time the physician may succeed in tiding her over the immediate consequences of the gonorrheal infection she innocently acquired. She may soon after become pregnant, and she may miscarry as a result of the old trouble, or she may carry the child the full period. When the child is born it may be blind and this defect is a consequence of the old infection to the mother from the father. If the mother is syphilitic the child most likely will inherit all the horrible possibilities of transmitted blood-poison.

Pregnancy frequently "lights up" any old, gonorrheal infection in the female, so this young wife fails to completely recover after the confinement. She is able to be about, but her strength refuses to be restored. It may be months later when she begins to suffer pain and to realize that she is quite sick. She develops a fever and may have a chill. The physician discovers that she has pus in her tubes and there is danger of peritonitis[Pg 149] or general blood poisoning. The old germs have been roused and are active. Unfortunately they are located where it is impossible to dislodge them without resorting to a serious operation. It is now a problem of saving her life. She is taken to the hospital and her womb, tubes, and ovaries, are removed—she is unsexed.

Young wives are being operated on every day, in every city in the civilized world for just such causes. It is a notorious fact, that, in every city in the world, the number of operations that are daily being performed on women, is increasing appallingly. Every surgeon knows that eighty per cent. of these operations are caused, directly or indirectly, by these diseases, and in almost every case in married women, they are obtained innocently from their own husbands. It is rare to find a married woman who is not suffering from some ovarian or uterine trouble, or some obscure nervous condition, which is not amenable to the ordinary remedies, and a very large percentage of these cases are primarily caused by infection obtained in the same way.

When a girl marries she does not know what fate has in store for her, nor is there any possible way of knowing, under the present marriage system. If she begets a sickly, puny child,—assuming she herself has providentially escaped immediate disease,—she devotes all her mother love and devotion to her child, but she is fighting a hopeless fight as I previously explained when I stated that one-half of the total effort of one-third of the race, is expended in combating conditions against which no successful effort is possible. Even her prayers are futile, because the wrong is implanted in the constitution of the child and the remedy is beyond her power to find. These are the tragedies of life, which no words may adequately describe, and compared to which the incidental troubles of the world at large are as nothing.

If the conditions are not as bad as those depicted above, the original infection may have rendered her sterile. If the germs reached the womb and tubes, the inflammatory process may close these tubes, with the result that conception is impossible. In these cases the woman has to bear the stigma and disgrace of a childless union, though[Pg 150] she is not the guilty party. Many husbands are sterile, however, as a result of venereal disease. It is claimed that eighty per cent. of childless marriages are caused by sterility of the male partner. Curiously and unfortunately these men never suspect themselves. The wife is the delinquent member, in their estimation. She is the victim of jest and suspicion, and later of jibes and insults. Many women have had their lives rendered miserable and unhappy because of this suspicion. They are compelled by their husbands to submit to examination and unpleasant and painful treatment and operations with the intention of rectifying a defective condition that does not exist. Many conscientious physicians refuse to treat women patients against whom the charge of sterility is made, before subjecting the husbands to thorough examination, and, since eighty per cent. of childless marriages are due to sterility in the male, this is a just and reasonable course to pursue.

During the course of all this domestic trouble and tragedy, the young wife's health has suffered—she scarcely enjoys one day of good health. Her mental condition is even worse. She submits to innuendo and insult under the impression that she is the unwitting cause of all the domestic wretchedness and often wishes she had never entered the marriage state. We must remember that these conditions wreck ideals and homes, and that they frequently render inefficient both husband and wife. The economic business of marriage becomes a failure, ambition is crushed and hope dies in the heart.

If the mother has been inoculated with the virus of syphilis her existence is equally wretched; her health is ruined; her efficiency is forever mortgaged. If she becomes pregnant she will most likely abort and she will go on aborting for years, in the effort to bring children into the home, accusing herself meantime and submitting to the reflections which are heaped upon her, while the real culprit is the husband. He assumes an injured and innocent attitude and behaves as if he had been imposed upon by marriage with a woman who cannot carry out her marital contract.

If she gives birth to a child or children, they are[Pg 151] syphilitic. They may be deformed, or they may be feeble-minded or idiots. They may live at home for years, always ailing, always sick. They may develop epilepsy, St. Vitus' dance, skin disease, or mental vagaries, and they may have to be put into institutions for the feeble-minded, or they may die by inches at home.

Is the Husband to Blame?—If a boy had gonorrhea a number of years before entering the marriage state, was treated for it by a physician, until all symptoms had disappeared and had enjoyed apparent good health in the interim, and had never been told any of the facts regarding probable consequences, is it just to blame him if he infects his wife? It is certain no man would willingly subject his bride to the risk of infection, with all its horrible consequences. These conditions exist as a result of the prudish attitude of society in the past toward all questions affecting sex hygiene. We have not told all the truth to the boy. Whatever knowledge he may have had was gained from companions, or from individuals who knew the garbled facts only. There is of course no excuse for the man who acquires disease after marriage and conveys it to his wife or children. This is a very different situation and one which should merit the severest condemnation and punishment. We are, however, only interested in the boy at present and will not take up the reader's time with a discussion of the "social evil" from this standpoint.

Building a Man.—When the boy is about fifteen years of age certain changes begin to manifest themselves. He grows more rapidly, a growth in which his whole system participates. His bones grow bigger and stronger, his muscles increase in size, even his heart, and lungs, and liver, and his digestive system accommodate themselves to this transformation; the voice changes and hair begins to grow on his face. The mental process also keeps pace with the new order of things. He thinks differently and he sees from a new viewpoint. Nature is making a man out of a boy.

These changes were not understood in the past, but we are beginning to appreciate the reason for this evolutionary process. We have discovered that the cause depends[Pg 152] upon certain active changes which take place in the sex organs. About this time the testicles begin to be active. For years these glands have been preparing themselves for this work, so they first grow rapidly, increasing in size until they are about eight times bigger than they were before this time, then they begin to pour into the circulation a secretion which stimulates changes in all other parts of the body and is directly responsible for the wonderful change that is evident in the stature of the boy's body.

This substance or "internal secretion" must not be confused with the semen. The internal secretion is simply the substance which nature employs in the developing process and is responsible for the degree of growth and quality of manhood which the boy manifests. The semen, on the other hand, is the procreative or fertilizing fluid which enables a man to beget offspring. When a boy understands this process it aids him in appreciating the importance of his sex organs and a little thought enables him to understand that if he abuses these organs he will seriously interfere with his own development. This process goes on for a number of years, until the boy reaches maturity. Any act or habit which weakens the quality of this secretion will deplete his powers and render him physically and mentally inefficient. To make a man, nature must be permitted to work in her own way. You cannot improve on her methods nor can you break her laws with impunity.

[Pg 153]

CHAPTER XIII

THE PARENTS AND THE BOY

Abuse of the Procreative Function—The Continent Life—Provide the Environment Necessary to the Clean Life—The Period of Procreative Power—Self-abuse—Masturbation—Treatment of Masturbation—Night Losses or Wet Dreams—Causes of Night Emissions—Sexual Excesses—Treatment of Sexual Excesses—What Parents Should Know About the So-called "Social Evil," Before Speaking with Authority to the Boy—The Need of Enlightenment in Sexual Matters—"No One Told Me, I Did Not Know"—Fake Medical Treatment of Venereal Diseases—Sowing Wild Oats—Should Circumcision be Advised?

Abuse of the Procreative Function.—Breeders of animals have discovered that to breed from very young stock is not good. The quality and stamina of the progeny is lowered and the vitality of the parent stock is reduced. It is not a good economic proposition.

Boys should therefore be taught that any form of sexual indulgence is harmful before the period of full growth.

Nature did not intend that the procreative function should be exercised by individuals who were not fully developed. The perpetuation of the species must not depend upon the license of immaturity. The instinct of sex-attraction must not be debased to serve a puerile, rather than a holy purpose.

Sexual indulgence in any form, and in any degree, at any age prior to full maturity is a perversion of the primal instinct of race perpetuation. The practice has a more intimate and a more personal association with growing boys, however, than a merely altruistic reference. Any indulgence of this character at this time is physically and mentally injurious. No boy can hope ever to acquire the full measure of his possible development as an efficient working or thinking machine if he wastes his vital[Pg 154] forces in unnatural liberties. He should be taught this truth in an emphatic manner by those responsible for his education.

There is a false idea prevalent that a continent life is harmful. So far as continence relates to immaturity, it may be strongly and justly asserted that it is probably the most important factor in the conservation of health and strength. The retention of the procreative fluids, at a time when nature is opposed to their loss, enables the growing economy to utilize them in the conservation of nervous energy and virility. If a boy dissipates these energizing fluids, he deprives his body of the richest products which he is capable of manufacturing at a time when he needs every aid in the building up of a physically and mentally sound and vigorous constitution. There cannot exist a normal development if the body is deprived of the essential ingredients necessary to growth and mental vigor.

There was a time when young men were actually taught that sexual intercourse was necessary to develop full manhood. This was followed by a period of silence, which has practically extended to recent times. Both of these systems are pernicious. We know that sexual intercourse is not necessary to the development of mature normal manhood or womanhood. On the contrary, we know that continence, not incontinence, is an absolute essential to the growth of full sexual, virile maturity, as well as to the growth of efficient and healthy manhood and womanhood.

We must appeal to a boy's reason and show him the personal side of clean living. When he understands that to attain success in every department of human effort,—on the baseball and football fields, in the ring, in gymnastic contents, in examinations, in social intercourse, in trades and professions,—a continent life is the only means possible that promises success, he will give the appeal consideration.

We must employ all the safety devices possible to guard against the inclination of youth to wander. Regular exercise is one of the very best institutions in this respect. If we can instill into our boys a love of manly[Pg 155] sports and encourage every effort in this direction, we will be doing much to minimize the growth of any tendency toward incontinence. We must provide the environment necessary to right living. The home should be attractive and we should permit the boy to have privileges even at the expense of the housekeeping decorum. His companions should be made welcome if they are the right kind of intimates, and the parents should enter into the life of the boy and try to look at "things" from his standpoint.

The Period of Procreative Power.—The procreative ability begins at puberty. There is no fixed period at which it may be said to end. From puberty until the period of physical maturity, it grows in vigor and it remains stationary until middle life, when it gradually declines. The standard of virility is unquestionably an individual problem. It depends upon the various factors that contribute to good health and longevity. It may be stated that the boy who abused his procreative function, during the period of immaturity, will not enjoy, during the mature period of his sexual life, a normal standard of vigor, nor will he carry the ability into old age, to the same relative degree, as he would, and as he had the innate promise to do—if he had led a normal continent existence. It may also be stated here that there is no effective remedial measures known, that will "bring back" the procreative ability if it is lost as a result of disobeying natural laws. Drugs and treatments by quacks to cure impotence are impositions and fakes. Money and time spent in the pursuit of this dream is money and time wasted.

Self-Abuse or Masturbation.—By self-abuse is meant the production of the venereal orgasm, with or without emission, by any means other than the natural union of the sexes.

It is a fact that the large majority of boys acquire the habit of self-abuse at some time. This is a very serious reflection upon parent, teacher, and physician, because it is through ignorance of the elementary principles of sex hygiene that this condition continues to exist. If they were warned against the possibility of[Pg 156] self-abuse arising in innocent ways, as well as in more reprehensible ways, they would exert their influence against its acquirement. If however a boy discovers accidentally a condition of which he was innocent, and of which he does not know the significance, it is human nature that he should investigate the phenomenon and in the end suffer as a consequence. In the effort to relieve some local irritation he may handle himself and be led into a dangerous practice. He does not know that the practice may have serious results—in fact he does not know he is doing anything wrong. Many boys have practically ruined their physical health and become morally irresponsible because no one—neither parent, teacher, physician, nor friend—told them of their danger. This is unjust, but great strides are being made in this direction and we may reasonably hope, that in the not far distant future, every boy will be plainly told the true facts about himself.

Most boys acquire this habit from other boys, but as we have intimated it is possible to acquire it in what are termed innocent ways. Sometimes the sensation which leads to it is discovered by sliding down banisters; or it may be that climbing trees or poles first awakens the feeling. Very young children are sometimes taught the vice by depraved nurses. Local irritation, as has been stated, may necessitate itching and handling the parts and in this way the vice is begun. The results are the same, no matter how the habit may have originated.

If the habit is persisted in, the muscular system suffers,—the muscles become weak and flabby; the patient develops weariness and languor and loses his mental and physical vigor. He is no longer forceful or energetic, his efficiency is impaired and as a consequence his nervous system begins to show signs of depleted strength. He cannot concentrate his thoughts, he falls behind in his studies, his mental effort is sluggish, he becomes diffident and shy, shuns society, loses confidence in himself, is morbid and emotional and may even think of suicide.

It is astonishing how indulgence in this habit may affect the moral nature of a boy. First of all, he is no longer frank and open. He becomes shifty and[Pg 157] suspicious and will not look you squarely in the face. A boy cannot become a slave to this habit without it affecting his mind. He invites debasing thoughts,—the old pure and clean method of thought and living no longer satisfy. His imagination even becomes corrupt and his moral nature and moral sense is perverted until he no longer seems to be able to tell the difference between right and wrong. He has little regard for the truth and if occasion demands it he will lie without appreciating the dishonorable part he is playing. In the end his will power is lost—even the effort to save himself is too feeble to succeed—he is a slave to the habit, his health and strength ruined.

If every boy could realize the possible end of this evil habit he would make an effort to rid himself of it before he becomes its victim and its slave. It may be easy to abandon the practice in the beginning. The longer he continues it, however, the less chance he has of finally mastering it, until, if he persists beyond a certain point, it is a matter of serious question whether he will ever be able to free himself from its grip. If the boy has lost the will power to carry out his resolves, no number of good desires or resolutions will avail. And it is just this will power that the wasting of the semen saps little by little away.

Treatment.—What can we do for these boys? Most of them can do much for themselves by simply stopping the practice. There are, of course, others who need careful management before the habit may be controlled and health restored. It is well to always remember to be tactful and patient and kind to these boys. Many of them are standing on the brink of despair, weak in body and weak in mind. They do not know where to turn to look for a friend—the right kind of a friend. It is a terrible thought that your own boy may be abjectly miserable in his own home because he is harboring a secret that is wrecking his health, and, though he may long for sympathy and a helping hand, neither his father nor mother have invited his confidence or spoken to him about these things. A watchful mother can usually tell when her boy becomes addicted to this habit.[Pg 158] He will show it in his manner, he will not be free and open, he will want to be by himself. Later he will show the effects of the abusive treatment he is subjecting himself to in his appearance. He will be sunken-eyed, pimply-faced, pasty-skinned, shiftless, sneaking, silent, unmanly. No mother can fail to note these signs and she should suspect the cause and take steps to tactfully reach him before he has ruined his health absolutely.

We would advise regular exercise of a vigorous kind. Tire out the body so that sleep may be sound. Cold baths, followed by brisk rub-downs; no intoxicants, light meals, plenty of drinking water morning and night. The bowels should be regular every day. He should sleep alone on a hard bed in a well-aired room with light covering. He should keep busy every minute of the day and he should not think of himself at all.

The boy must realize that his salvation rests with himself. After he knows the real danger which the habit carries with it, he must be on his guard every moment to abstain. If he does not he may rest assured that the practice will ruin his health, render him, a business failure and deprive him of all happiness during the rest of his life.

Night Losses or "Wet-Dreams."—A so-called wet-dream is an unconscious emission of semen during sleep. The discharge may or may not be accompanied with an erotic dream.

After a certain age—which may be from the twelfth or fourteenth year—a boy may discover that he has discharged some substance during his sleep. He finds the discharge on his night clothes and it naturally puzzles him greatly. He may be entirely unconscious of the whole proceeding, having slept soundly during the night, or he may wake up to find the fluid actually discharging.

If a boy has not been told of this phenomenon he may regard it as a form of self-abuse of which he may have heard and as a consequence he may worry himself sick, as the night emissions continue to occur from time to time. Many pure-minded boys have been rendered miserable, and their efficiency and health have suffered as[Pg 159] a result of just such an experience. It is, therefore, proper that they should fully understand the true significance of these occurrences.

Causes of Night Emissions.—I have explained how nature makes a man out of a boy. During this maturing process the testicles are very active organs—their function is to manufacture or secrete the fertilizing fluid or semen. This maturing process begins actively, as I stated, about the age of fifteen, though in some boys it frequently occurs earlier, sometimes as early as the twelfth year. When the testicle begins to grow at this time they manufacture more semen than the little pockets can hold, so nature adopts the method of permitting the surplus to escape during sleep. These night emissions, therefore, are perfectly natural losses, and need cause absolutely no distress of mind whatever. The frequency with which they may occur depends altogether upon the temperament of the boy. If the boy is a strong, active, athletic boy, they may not be so frequent in him as they may be in a quiet, studious boy. The system of the athletic boy seems to utilize more of this surplus than the quieter existence of the studious boy calls for. If the discharge does not occur oftener than once every two weeks, it may be regarded as normal and natural. Should they become more frequent than this, the boy should inform his mother or father and the family physician should be consulted. It may be that he is in need of a tonic, or special instructions regarding his method of living and his mode of exercising. Whatever the cause may be, it can be corrected, and the best plan is to give it attention as soon as it is noted that the losses are too frequent.

Sexual Excesses.—It is well known to the medical profession that the marital relation is frequently practiced to excess. The same indictment may be passed on what may be termed extra-marital relations. No one has ever formulated a general sexual standard which could be safely regarded as normal. Too many individual conditions of temperament and health enter into the proposition to permit of a standard being formulated. It must, therefore, be regarded as an individual question[Pg 160] to be adjusted, if necessary, by the family physician. What may safely be regarded as normal and harmless in one, constitutes, for many reasons, excess in another. When a man performs hard physical or mental labor, his sexual aptitude or capacity is limited, and this limitation cannot be exceeded without risk. Such a limitation may not constitute an excess in a man whose occupation does not call for a great expenditure of physical or mental energy. Any indulgence which produces exhaustion is excessive.

The age of the individual has undoubtedly much to do with his sexual endurance. A young, virile adult will tolerate a sexual expenditure which would seriously affect the health and vigor of an older man.

Environment and inclination are factors in determining the standard of some people. If the marital relations are participated in simply to preserve peace and harmony in the home, they are productive of harm even if indulged in moderately.

The symptoms of sexual excess are much the same as those of self-abuse. To a certain extent, however, they are favorably influenced, because the conditions under which the relationship is practiced are natural, because the participants are matured physically, and because there is no element of worry over the probable effects.

Sexual excess defeats its own purpose, because it engenders a lack of desire and consequently it is to a certain extent a self-limiting process. We must also remember that excess entails consequences just as the breaking of any natural law is followed by retribution of some kind. In these cases we find that discomfort follows excess. The parts become irritated and congested and disease of the prostate gland always follows.

Treatment.—Stop the excess by self-control and self-restraint. Employ all the aids dictated by an intelligent perusal of the laws of sex hygiene. Preserve the general health. It may be necessary to resort to local treatment, because, if the parts have been abused by excessive indulgence, there is always more or less irritation and congestion present. This condition affects the nerves, suggestive reflex sensations are produced by a congested[Pg 161] prostate and the patient becomes morbid. It is essential for such patients to consult a physician whose local treatment will stop the sensitiveness in the parts and relieve him so that he may carry out his programme of restoration unhampered by conditions which are only amenable to local treatment.

What Parents Should Know About the So-Called "Social Evil" Before Speaking With Authority to "The Boy."—To be qualified to speak with authority, or convincingly, to a boy upon sex hygiene, the parents must be familiar with, and well versed in the subject. The facts related in the preceding pages must be thoroughly understood. No parent can study these facts intelligently without being impressed with the importance of the subject; without realizing that it is absolutely essential that the fundamental principles of sex hygiene should be taught to the rising generation; without acknowledging the tremendous part for evil which prudery and ignorance play in the education of youth; and without being convinced that most of the evil is the product of ignorance on the part of the boy, and that parents are in a large sense to blame if they fail to impart the necessary knowledge in time.

The need for enlightenment in sexual matters is a product of existing conditions. Civilization and the social environment are developing along a plane which subjects the youth to temptations that practically did not exist in the past. There is a broader and looser code of ethics. Business monopolizes the entire time of the father, and social and political unrest and misdirected ambition distracts the mother. The son or daughter has a wider latitude and a freer reign than they once had. The opportunities for promiscuous intimacies are easier, and the public conveniences and utilities lend themselves to the designs of evil-intentioned and loose-moraled women. The ease of travel, the laxity of laws, the theater, with its unchaste and indecent plays, the moving picture snows, the vaudeville resorts, whose highest priced "talent" is some voluptuous female, who has cultivated the art of draping nudity with suggestiveness and singing immoral songs, all tend to give youth a false impression[Pg 162] of the reality of life and to make the path of the degenerate easy and profitable. The rich are growing richer, and their children are pampered and overfed and underrestrained. Time hangs heavily on their hands and their only mental effort is to devise new methods and new ways of satisfying the lust of liberty and overstimulated desire. The poor are growing poorer, and to "keep in the ring," to live and dress beyond their means as many do, it is necessary to have an unexacting standard of morals. In this way the promiscuous libertine is evolved,—the most insidious and dangerous product of present day civilization, and the most pernicious factor in the spread of immoral impulses and indecent diseases.

Parents must accept these institutions and agencies as necessary instruments of evil and adopt measures to nullify their attractiveness. Eternal vigilance is the price of success, but the quality of the vigilance must be dictated by love, not by suspicion and distrust.

When the parent can convince the boy that the knowledge is imparted, not with the intention of depriving him of what he may construe as his natural liberties and rights, but with the single intention of adding to the sum total of his pleasure and success, he will look more kindly upon any proposition that suggests a course of conduct that leads to clean living. Sex hygiene will eventually find a natural place in the scheme of education. It will be taught to male and female alike. In the meantime, however, we must begin by educating the educators—the parents. In the beginning, their task will not be easy. There will be much to overcome, much ignorance, prudery, false modesty, hypocrisy; there will be much vicious teaching and evil example to live down. But we cannot hope to achieve results in the noblest cause, save by patient, intelligent, and persistent effort and by self-sacrifice and a constant enthusiasm. The aim is to tell all,—all the truth,—so that we may never be assailed by the cry, "No one told me, I did not know," from the loved lips of son or daughter gone astray.

The Father and the Boy.—The right kind of father can always find the time and the way to awaken in the heart of the boy the spirit of companionship. No boy[Pg 163] living will resent the fellowship of the right kind of father. It depends upon the father! If the spirit of chumminess does not exist between you and your boy, you are at fault, you have made a mistake, you have missed your opportunity, you "did not go about it in the right way and in the right spirit." Try again—it may not be too late.

The father who adopts the habit of taking his boys (and his girls too) out for long walks, at least every Sunday, and who spends an hour with them every evening—is the right kind of father. One who has never tested the merit of walks with children cannot possibly appreciate the enjoyment and benefit that can accrue from them. It is not only the physical good that results, nor the inspiration which one may draw from nature, but the concrete advantages that come from the fellowship with the children are a new and a real experience—this is what counts. You will have opportunities of sewing seeds in their minds that will grow into a harvest that will astonish you. Children in the right mood—and they are in the right mood when they are happy, and they are happy out in the open with an interesting companion—are alert, and responsive, and eager to be told "things," and this mood can be put to marvelous use by the "right kind of father." The father who wanders forth with the fixed purpose of thinking out some business problem during the walk and permits the children to find their own amusement is the wrong kind of father. He must choose to be a child again, he must desire to please them, he must make an effort to be in harmony with them, he must draw on his experience to interest them, he must talk to them entertainingly of every interesting problem which the walk itself suggests or he must formulate a plan and select a subject with a definite educational scheme in view. We can, in a most effective way, begin to build their characters, and, by the right kind of talk and enthusiasm, he can determine their resolves to be honest, truthful, just, clean, sympathetic. He can instill into them, in a thousand different ways, the determination and inspiration to succeed. It is a wonderful and a precious chance, and it will make the "right kind of father" more just,[Pg 164] more sympathetic, more optimistic, and it will make him young again and more successful. Try it.

Implant in the hearts of your children a love of home, make the evening meal and hour by the fireside a period of congenial fellowship, when all the little irritable ruffles of the day may be ironed out and swept away. The secret is to be intimate. Tell them the secret of success from your standpoint, how happiness is gained only by being efficient and successful, and that, to be efficient, one must be energetic and healthy. Drum into their ears the truth that life is a battle, and only the brave "win out," and health is the one essential necessity. It is astonishing how such talks will impress young minds. They will remind you of things you said, that made a lasting impression on them, long after you have forgotten the incident.

A father can, in this way, by talking of the future to his boy, convey to him the high hopes he entertains of the great success the boy is going to achieve—you establish a standard in the boy's mind, and he unconsciously hopes to attain that standard. If you have impressed him with the necessity of preserving his health and strength, as an essential to success, he will be slow to yield to any temptation that may interfere with his plans. This reasoning may sound quixotic to some people, but it is the truth. Many a boy has been inspired to success by the knowledge that his mother or father believed in him, and was confident he would be a leader. He strove to justify the pride and confidence of those who held him dear, and he won out.

To retain his health, therefore, is the first impulse to be conveyed to the boy. When he recognizes this truth, it is an easy task to instill a love of exercise, gymnastics, swimming, fresh air, cleanliness and temperance in him. If these are attained, you will have tided him over the tendency to self-abuse, and you will have rendered him less likely to yield to evil suggestion or temptation. His confidence in you will be whole-hearted and implicit. You can do anything with him at the psychological moment. It is now time to talk of more intimate matters. Carefully and tactfully, the father approaches the fundamental truths of sex hygiene.[Pg 165]

The selection of a subject for a text as a means from which to advance toward the real facts is sometimes of importance. It must not appear as though the subject was designedly chosen. If it follows in a natural way it will more thoroughly interest the boy and he will have swallowed a large dose of truth before he is impressed with the personal viewpoint. A passing trotting horse has served me a number of times for intimate talks with boys on heredity and kindred subjects. I invite the boy to watch how the horse uses his legs, and how rhythmically and beautifully he places his feet, and how his whole attitude serves the end for which he is exerting himself—to gain speed. Tell the boy the story of how professional breeders have achieved such marvelous results; how for generations the "strain" has been kept clean and pure, how any descendant of a great sire, who showed any habit detrimental to the development of the highest racing qualities—no matter how trivial the disability might be—was cast aside, experience having taught that it does not pay to waste effort and time on any horse whose physical or mental characteristics are not up to the highest standard. Such a horse will not win, and it is only "wins" that count.

Change the subject to human beings. Tell him how the race maintains its standard; but show him the difference between the methods employed. How the horse has his mate selected because of the female's good qualities, so that the offspring may possess like qualities, if not better, and that the selection is made by men who know their business, and have had long experience in the work. How, on the other hand, a young man with no experience is permitted to choose any woman he may fancy irrespective of her qualifications. As a consequence, we have all kinds of children, good and bad, feeble and strong, honest and dishonest, some degenerates from birth, some criminal, and many diseased and inefficient, few of them "winners." It is an easy matter to preach a little sermon from this text. Show him how essential it is to select the mother of one's children wisely, to know if there is disease in the future wife's blood, if her family history is good, if her temperament is suited to his, if her[Pg 166] domestic qualities are satisfactory, if her principles are moral and normal, and if she understands and appreciates the true object and function of marriage. Show him also the element of justice involved in the marriage contract; that he must give what he exacts, that if he expects a healthy and normal wife, he must be healthy and normal himself; if he expects purity and cleanliness he must give purity and cleanliness; if he expects to mate with a fit female he must be an efficient and fit male. Remember that every act, deed, thought, and aspiration is regulated by laws which one cannot fool with, or disobey, without reaping a harvest which will conquer, crush and ruin you, no matter how clever or smart you may think yourself.

Show him the wisdom of the breeders' habit of never permitting sexual liberties in a too young stallion. For the same reason the boy must conserve his strength and virility for the marriage state and for the function of procreation.

In a further talk, the father may extend this subject and gradually lead up to the "consequences" of the unclean life. The boy will be ready for this talk and will evince an interest in it that will be encouraging and promising.

The talk about the science of mating the horses he will understand readily and thoroughly, and he will not fail to see the point when you switch to man and apply the same principles. Then when you show how mismating is responsible for poor children quality and how disease accounts for feeble-minded and degenerate offspring, he will be fairly well posted, and he will be ready to imbibe more details, and you will have done much of your duty. His curiosity will be quickened and his interest is awakened. It depends upon the father. If your boy is honest and clean, open and decent, he will not fall without a fight, and while he is fighting he is maturing. If your picture of the consequences of the venereal diseases has been effective and vivid, he will grow up with a healthy horror of them. If your conduct as a father has been wise and exemplary, and if your home has the right kind of environment, and the right kind of mother in it, you[Pg 167] have done all a father can do to help the boy over the rough spots. The proper kind of encouragement and the right kind of vigilance, and books which will satisfy the boy's craving for more knowledge along this line is all that is needed to help the boy to "win out."

Fake Medical Treatment for Venereal Diseases.—Parents should in every possible way discourage the use of patent medicines and fake medical methods of curing these diseases. Untold harm has been done to boys and to women by these nostrums.

In every instance the motive underlying the methods of people selling these things is to frighten the patients into the belief that their condition is more serious than it is in order to justify a long and expensive course of treatment.

Their work is carelessly performed, and frequently they are directly responsible for the development of complication and dangerous sequelæ. The promises of speedy cures are false, and, not infrequently, methods of black-mailing have been known to follow an expensive and unsuccessful course of treatment.

There is no class of disease in which the help and honesty of the legitimate medical profession is needed more than in the treatment of the venereal diseases. Parents should see to it that the family physician is prescribing any strange medicine that may appear in the boy's room, and not some unknown individual who may be an impostor and a blackmailer.

Sowing Wild Oats.—Writers of fiction and others of a more serious trend of thought have recognized the sowing of wild oats as an institution which, if it does not merit the full approval of society's moral code, is, at least, tolerated. No serious consequences befall the offender. On the contrary, the libertine is the type of hero who receives the commendatory quips of erotic dames and the questionable interest of hysterical maidens.

Women of easy morals are always willing to espouse the cause of the "black sheep," and to further the matrimonial success of the penitent *roué*. Many mothers are willing to marry their daughters to the polished villain of society, who is known as a rake and debauchee, if his[Pg 168] family connections are desirable. It has been even held that a youth who did not "sow his wild oats" was of doubtful stamina.

That many able men have sown wild oats is indisputable, and that many men who are respectful husbands, have also gone "through the mill" is also true, but this need not blind us to the fact that thousands upon thousands, who could have been successful men of affairs and creditable husbands and fathers, have been utterly ruined, as a result of having sown wild oats. No man is a better man because of a past record of licentious habits. The man who sows and escapes the harvest is lucky. The man who reaps, reaps in abundance. Most men regret the lapses of youth. Most of these lapses would never have occurred if the impulse could have been governed by the reasoning of maturity. These acts are the promptings of an impetuosity which may be entirely foreign to the individual's innate character, but brought out by promiscuous circumstances and the ignorance and license of youth. If we can protect youth, by an adequate knowledge of the consequences, we will furnish the means to tide over the impressionable period. Until a healthy maturity of judgment will assume the task unaided.

The effects of the wild oats' theory are too tragically evident to need any argumentative refutation. The statistics of the prevalency of venereal diseases alone is sufficient; the results of these diseases are more than enough.

Study the records of the jails and prisons, courts and asylums, hospitals and health resorts, think of the hundreds of thousands of diseased and deformed and mentally inferior children, of the multitude of paretics, melancholies, ataxics, maniacs, syphilitics,—all the products of "wild oats,"—and ask if the wild oats' theory is justifiable.

Think of the ruined homes, the wretched lives of fallen women, the hopeless prayers of abandoned wives, the loneliness and misery of parents neglected and forgotten, the "bastards" and fatherless children, the drunkards and criminals and tramps—all weeds of the wild oats' harvest.[Pg 169]

Then reflect upon the tragedies, the suicides of the betrayed and of the diseased, the bank thief, the broken hearts of deserted and hungry children, the army of inefficients—around whose necks hang wild oats' medals, the men of big business, who constantly fight the effects of early incontinence and abuse, and the thousands who go to early graves, and then ask, in all justice, if the sowing of wild oats needs justification.

Who supports the thousands of prostitutes? Who made them? Wherever you find pauperism, crime, drunkenness, insanity, idleness, immorality, vice and disease, you will find that the sower of wild oats has traveled the path and left his stain and his footprints there.

Should Circumcision be Advised?—The answer to the above question is "Yes," in every instance. If circumcision is done early,—during the first two weeks of life,—the operation is without danger and practically without pain. In quite a considerable percentage of all males, circumcision is an absolute necessity. For excellent medical reasons, about which your family physician can inform you, every boy should be circumcised.

[Pg 173]

CHAPTER XIV

A MOTHER'S DUTY TO HER DAUGHTER

What a Mother Should Tell Her Little Girl—Where Do Babies Come From—How Baby Birds and Fish Come from Eggs—How Other Animals Have Little Nests of Their Own—The Duty of Mothers to Instruct and Direct—What a Mother Should Tell Her Daughter—Every Mother Should Regard This Duty as Sacred—Every Female Child is a Possible Future Mother—Motherhood the Highest Function of the Sex—Health the One

Necessary Essential—Symptoms of the First, or Beginning Menstruation—The Period of Puberty in the Female—Changes in the Reproductive Organs at Puberty—The Female Generative Organs—The Function of the Reproductive Organs—The Age of Puberty in the Female—The Function of the Ovary—The Function of the Womb—Why Menstruation Occurs Every Twenty-eight Days—The Male or Papa Egg—The Function of the Spermatozoa—"Tell the Whole Story"—"How do These Spermatozoa Get There"—The Union of the Species—"How Can a Baby Live in There for Such a Long Time"—How the Baby Gets its Nourishment in the Womb—Girls Must Not Become Mothers.

What a Mother Should Tell Her Little Girl.—Every little girl should be told the Story of Life by her mother. It should be told in simple language, so that the little girl will understand. Very early in life the little girl will be prompted to inquire of her mother "Where do babies come from?" It is wrong to give an evasive reply to this natural inquiry or to postpone telling the story, because they will be told it by playmates and will receive very wrong and very crude impressions of this wonderful subject.

Every mother knows enough of life to tell her little girl its story in a way that will impress her with the sacredness of God's beautiful reproductive plan. She should begin by telling her a story about how the birds live. How at a certain season of the year they choose a mate[Pg 174] and go housekeeping. They build a nest, and when it is all nicely finished, the mother bird lays her eggs. Then the papa and mamma bird take turns and sit on the eggs to keep them warm, and after a time the egg breaks and a little bird is born into the world. They feed the little baby birds until their feathers grow, and when they are old enough they fly away from their home and begin life by themselves.

Many questions will be asked as the mother tells the story in her own words, and the correct answers to these questions will fill in all the difficult-to-understand points. The story of how the fish lay eggs in shallow water so that the sun may keep them warm and hatch them out will interest also. Be careful to impress upon them that there is always a mamma and a papa, a male and a female bird and fish,—that this is necessary because God made it so, and we must obey His wish. When the little girl fully understands the story of the egg bird, and egg fish, the mother can tell how the Creator thought out a different plan for other animals like the dog, horse, lion, elephant, and cow. He knew that it would neither be safe nor possible for these animals to stay at home long enough to sit on eggs and hatch their babies, so he made a nest for them inside of their bodies. There they would be warm and would always be with their mammas no matter what they were doing. So we come to the answer to their question: "Where do babies come from?"

These interesting stories, according to the intelligence and sincerity of the mother, can be taken advantage of, to impress the little girl with the importance of many of the lessons of life. For example, her attention can be drawn to the fact that man and woman are the highest types of living things that God made. No other living thing, animal, or fish, or bird, or tree, or flower, can talk, and think, and reason as man and woman can. Because of this faculty—to think and reason—the human family are always trying to find out what can be done with all the other things God made. We try to find out what the different rocks are good for; what the different trees are good for, and the different kinds of earth, and animals, and birds, and fishes, and everything in the world. We[Pg 175] study these, and we learn much, and we are made happier and more comfortable by what we learn. For example, by studying horses, and feeding and breeding them carefully, and training them, and caring for them, we can make stronger horses and better and faster horses; by studying trees, and planting them in soil best suited to them, and giving them plenty of water to drink, we can compel these trees to grow better apples and pears and peaches. In the same way we can produce better strawberries, and oranges, and grapes, and we can grow flowers with sweeter smells and prettier colors. We do all this by training these animals and trees to grow a certain way, to eat certain food, to drink pure water, and we protect them from the cold and sometimes from the sun if it is too hot. Our faculty to think and reason has taught us just what is good for them, and we compel them to obey our laws. As a result they become strong and more healthy. Now show the little girl how important she is; how much more precious she is than a tree, or animal, or flower, and how much more necessary it is that we, mammas and papas, should use our ability to think and reason in her interest.

Show her how we have found out all about babies and little girls and how we know just what to do to make strong and healthy, and pure, and good, and clean men and women of all the little boys and girls in the world. Tell her that this is what mother is doing now, training her and compelling her to do the things that will make her a strong and a good mother when she grows older. Let her distinctly understand that it is the duty of mothers to instruct and to correct their little daughters when they do any wrong. Mothers know, because they have had experience in these matters, and they know just how a little girl must live, and dress, and eat, and behave, in order to be strong and pure, and good. So when mother reproves and corrects, it is because she knows that what you are doing to merit a correction is not for your ultimate good. Show them that all young things, and young animals, and young babies, and young girls, must be compelled to obey certain rules and laws, otherwise they would not grow up to be strong and healthy. Sometimes a rose bush grows up among[Pg 176] stones and weeds, but it never thrives, it is always more or less sick. It does not grow strong, its flowers are poor little sickly things compared to the roses on a bush that is planted in proper soil, and carefully tended and pruned, and watered. So would the little girl turn out if she grew up in bad company and did not have a mother to guard and guide her,—to prune her when she was growing careless. Everything in this world has a meaning, and when mother tells you that you must not do a certain thing you very much want to do, she has a very good reason for telling you not to do it. You may not know the reason, but you should have confidence in your mother, you should believe that she knows what is best, and that she would not inflict pain or cause you suffering unless she knew it was for your good. The young horse does not understand why a halter is put around its neck and is made to run around in a circle until it is tired. It would much rather enjoy itself in its own care-free, and happy way. And when finally a full set of harness is put on, and it is put into the shafts of a wagon and tied there, and made to pull it and its driver many weary miles the horse does not like it, and he rebels strenuously. He is, however, compelled to obey in the end, and he finally consents to become a useful horse.

It is exactly the same way with every little boy and girl. We are put into this world for a certain purpose, and we must all work. Now parents know this, and they know just how to prepare little girls and boys for this work. They therefore ask them to do many things that are not pleasant or agreeable but which must be done in order to prepare them for the work ahead.

WHAT A MOTHER SHOULD TELL HER DAUGHTER

Your daughter is now about fourteen years of age. She is about to pass from girlhood to womanhood and she should know more of life's story. The mother will now tell her the complete story in the form of little talks, based upon the following facts as texts. Each mother will doubtless add to the story as conditions justify and as the education of the mother and daughter may dictate. A multitude of little side talks can be wisely indulged in[Pg 177] to make clear any uncertain or doubtful explanation, and every one of these incidental excursions can be made exceedingly interesting if wisely and opportunely chosen. Always remember, however, to emphasize the sacredness of the story. Do not permit your daughter to get the impression that you are telling her something that simply has to be told, just as you told her the correct way to boil an egg. Let her realize and get the impression that this is the most serious and most wonderfully interesting story in existence, the most important story she will ever hear. Let her understand that motherhood, for which she is now preparing, is the duty God assigned her in this world: that that duty must be carried out, and that she must do nothing, nor leave anything undone, to interfere with its accomplishment. Do not only impress her with the story itself, but let your own explanation be so emphatically serious, that she will deeply appreciate its momentous significance—an occasion to be remembered all her life.

If she gets the proper impression from you at this time she will never treat the subject lightly, or permit it to be promiscuously discussed within her hearing.

Begin by telling her that she is about to enter the most important period of her life. Explain why this is so in the following way, in your own words. If we admit every female child to be a future mother, and motherhood the highest function possible to the sex, then the awakening of the sex organs and the mother instinct, must be the most important developmental episode in the life story of every woman. If this is so, then it follows that every girl should enter this period in the very best physical health possible, in order to reap the best results incident to this evolutionary period. We impress and warn her, therefore, that, as her system is about to undergo important changes, she must be particularly careful of her health. A little mistake at this time may be followed by more serious consequences than if made at any other time in her life. If a girl is to become a mother, certain changes must occur in her body before the nest, of which we previously wrote, can be made ready. God did not overlook anything when He peopled the earth; He therefore[Pg 178] wisely planned that these changes in the female should occur at a time when the girl is strong and healthy.

The Period of Puberty in the Female. Symptoms of Beginning Menstruation.—At about the age of fourteen these changes begin to give evidence of existence. They affect the girl's whole system and the mother must be especially patient and sympathetic. Her disposition may change, she may want to be alone, and she may be more or less melancholy. She will be dissatisfied with the things that previously interested her. She will tire easily, and she may have many spasmodic pains from time to time. The wise mother will tactfully see that she takes plenty of nourishing food and systematic exercise, and that she gets enough sleep in a well-aired room. There are other physical changes which are observable at this age. The girl grows taller, the figure broadens out, the hips widen, the bust enlarges, and the waist line increases in size. These are all part of the great change from girlhood to womanhood.

Changes in the Reproductive Organs.—The principal change takes place in the reproductive organs themselves, and it is very essential that she should have a clear mental picture of just what is meant by "reproductive" organs and their location in her body. We mean by this term the group of organs which are concerned in creating and nourishing a child until it is old enough to be born into the world.

The Female Generative Organs.—These organs are the womb or uterus, two ovaries, two fallopian tubes and the vagina. The womb or uterus is the "nest." It is about the size of and is shaped like a pear. It is hollow, however, though its walls are quite thick. The ovaries are about the size of a peach stone and lie at the side of the womb,—one on either side. The fallopian tubes connect the ovaries with the womb. The vagina connects the womb with the outside world,—it is sometimes known as the birth canal. In the very lowest part of the abdomen, or belly, in front, is the bladder, which collects the urine until it is necessary to pass it out. In the back part of this region is the rectum; it collects all the undigested food, etc., from the intestinal canal.[Pg 179] Between these two,—the bladder and rectum,—we find the reproductive organs, the womb, ovaries and vagina, described above.

The Function of the Reproductive Organs.—It will be difficult, even for mothers, to acquire a clear understanding of the function of the reproductive or generative organs. It is an exceedingly interesting process, however, and it is well worth a patient, attentive study to clearly understand the brief description we give of it. If you acquire a distinct mental picture of the problem you will be able to tell your daughter a story that will be of intense interest to her, and a tale that is interesting is impressive and is productive of thought and reflection. That is the condition of mind we want daughters to be in when they hear this story.

The human ovaries begin to prepare themselves for their life work when the girl is about eight years of age. When they are ripe, or ready to perform this duty, the girl menstruates for the first time. This is known as the age of "puberty," which implies that she has developed, passed from girlhood into womanhood. After having reached the age of puberty it is possible to become a mother.

The Age of Puberty.—There is no fixed age at which the first menstruation takes place. Some girls develop quicker than others,—a condition that depends upon the health and type of girl. A strong, robust, full-blooded girl will menstruate at an earlier age, than will a sickly anemic girl. The average age is fourteen years, though there is no reason to worry if a girl does not menstruate for a number of years later. In warm climates the age of puberty is from two to four years earlier than in more temperate climates.

The Function of the Ovary.—Just what takes place in each ovary when it is ripe is best explained by likening an ovary to an orange,—though of course the ovary is very much smaller than an orange, as was previously noted. If you make a cut in an orange and squeeze it, you express some of its juice and most likely you will also express one or more seeds. The seeds of the ovaries are called "ovules," and the process by which it expresses[Pg 180] them is called "ovulation." Of course there is no actual squeezing of the ovary,—the ovules grow in the ovary, and as they ripen they come to the surface, and when actually ripe, the part of the surface of the ovary to which they come, opens up (like a flower unfolding when in bloom), and they fall out. The ovule we may regard as the human female egg, and one ripens and falls out every twenty-eight days.

When the egg falls out of the ovary it falls into the tube which carries it into the womb. This tube you will remember is called the fallopian tube. The ovule or egg is now in the cavity of the womb where we will leave it for the present.

The Function of the Womb.—While these changes are going on in the ovary, the womb is also preparing itself for its share of the work. The lining or internal surface of the womb is composed of mucous membrane, much the same as the interior lining of the mouth and throat. This lining becomes congested with blood, and is so intensely swollen at the time when the ovule or egg reaches the womb, that it is ready to rupture and bleed all over its surface. Just whether it will rupture and bleed, depends upon whether the egg is going to grow into a child or not. If it is not going to grow into a child, it immediately bleeds freely, and continues to bleed, until the whole lining of the womb and egg is passed out into the outer world. This takes four or five days and constitutes "menstruation." After menstruation is over, the womb begins again to prepare itself for the coming of the next ovule or egg, and as this occurs every twenty-eight days, menstruation is commonly termed the "monthly periods."

Why Menstruation Occurs Every Twenty-Eight Days.—The reason why the womb does this every twenty-eight days is because it is impossible to tell just when the womb will be called upon to nourish and support a child. If it did not get rid of the old blood, it would not be in a healthy condition to nourish and take care of a baby, nor would its interior be ready to supply new fresh blood for the growth of the infant. Hence nature constructs and builds a new "nest" in the interior[Pg 181] of the womb each month. It very much resembles the new home into which the bride and groom, go to begin housekeeping.

When you told your little girl the story of life, you particularly drew her attention to the important fact that every living thing is created by the union of a male and female principle, and, therefore, has a mamma and papa. This applies to trees, flowers, vegetables, fish, animals, birds, insects,—every living thing, including human beings. We have seen that the ovule from the ovary is the female egg, or principle. It is the part the female contributes toward the future child. Before a child is possible, however, the ovule must meet the egg from the male.

The Male or Papa Egg.—The male or papa egg is called a "spermatozoa." It reaches the interior of the womb through the lower opening, which you will remember opens into the vagina. Emphasize to your daughter that the female ovule or egg, and the male egg, or spermatozoa, are minute objects, so microscopically small that a hundred million of them could comfortably lie upon a ten-cent piece.

The Function of the Spermatozoa.—God gave the male spermatozoa the power to move. To watch them under the microscope you would imagine you were looking into a bowl of water, in which there were hundreds of little fish all squirming around. But the most wonderful thing about them is, they can only move in an upward direction,—they seemingly cannot move downward, or sideways. If you think for a moment you will understand why God gave them this marvelous property. When the male semen is deposited in the female vagina, there are thousands of these minute, living, moving spermatozoa in it. The womb is above the vagina, and the female egg is in the womb, consequently, to reach this egg, the spermatozoa must travel upward. To travel in any other direction would be fruitless energy. There is only one female egg, but there are thousands of male eggs, or spermatozoa; it is easy, therefore, to comprehend how one of these spermatozoa should exactly be in line with the female egg in its upward path, since there are so[Pg 182] many of them. It is only necessary that one should meet the female egg in order to impregnate it.

The shape of the male principle, or spermatozoa, is exactly like a little tadpole, and you no doubt recall that a tadpole has a minute tail, the movement of which enables it to swim around. So has the spermatozoa, and by the incessant movement of this microscopic tail they all move upward as soon as discharged by the male. I told you that God gave the male-germ life. It is necessary now to explain the character of this life. It is very brief; it is estimated that they are active for two hours, and then become inactive, or die. The best way to explain the brief activity to your daughter, is to liken the spermatozoa, to a mechanical toy, which is wound up to go for a certain time. After it runs out it becomes inactive; this is exactly what happens to the little human tadpole. If during this brief life none of them has happened to reach the female egg, pregnancy does not take place and menstruation occurs. On the other hand, if this were not so,—if these spermatozoa were active for a longer period, pregnancy would almost be certain to take place every time the womb was not already occupied with a pregnancy.

Tell the Whole Story.—When a mother reaches this stage of the wondrous tale she will be asked by an innocent girl,—"How do these spermatozoa get there?" or, "You have not told me where these tadpoles came from" or, "I don't understand how these spermatozoa got into the vagina" or, "I don't know why you call these the male egg when they are in mamma." It does not matter how it is expressed, the intent is plain enough. I have said, that an innocent girl will ask this question, the implication being that one who is not innocent will refrain from asking this question. A girl who knows the answer will not ask, because, if she is familiar with this subject before her mother thinks it wise and proper to tell her, she obtained her information from a source which, most likely, insinuated a suggestive, or evil, meaning into the explanation, consequently she would be afraid, or ashamed, to ask the question. An innocent girl, on the other hand, would rightly ask for information which[Pg 183] is obviously kept back, and which she has a right to know, since a complete, and intelligent understanding of the story depends upon the elucidation asked. If it is proper to tell part of the story, it is essential to tell all of it. Tell it in your own words in this way:

When God conceived the human race He ensured its perpetuation by designing a method whereby this would be rendered possible: He did more; He wisely decided that the function, involving the very existence of the human race, should be attended with a sentient gratification. He further instilled into the fundamental economy of mankind, sex attraction, which is involuntary, undeniable, and unquenchable. If God conceived the means and the method, no human mind in possession of its faculties should see evil where it does not exist. It was by Him designed that the male organ of reproduction should deposit its germinating fluid in the vagina of the female, and this is accomplished by a union of species.

The one set of reproductive organs is a complement of the other, and essential to the other. It is by this act that the male spermatozoa is enabled to complete the function of fecundation.

If now we assume the male and female element to have met and united, menstruation does not take place. The egg or embryo (the future child) begins to grow, and it remains in the womb for two hundred and eighty days from the day when the male and female egg met. It is quite natural for an intelligent girl to ask her mother to explain, "How a baby can live in there for such a long time," or "What makes it grow if it does not get anything to eat or drink."

How the Baby Gets its Nourishment in the Womb.—These questions can be answered in this way. While the baby is in its little comfortable home it gets everything it needs. You are in your home now. If you wanted a drink, what would you do? Wouldn't you go to the water faucet and draw a glass of water? The water comes to you through a pipe, right into your home, you don't have to go out of the house to get it. And if you wanted light when it is dark you would turn on the gas and light it. It, too, comes into your home through[Pg 184] a pipe. Now baby gets its air; and food, and all it needs to drink in just that way. There are two little pipes which go into its nest or home, and then into the baby's body at the navel, and through these pipes fresh blood runs in and out. When mother breathes, her blood sucks up oxygen from the air in her lungs, and the blood carries oxygen to every part of her body. In this way, all parts are supplied with the proper quantity of air. Now the baby is simply a new part of mamma as long as it is in its nest in her body, so it too gets air in this way. When mother eats, the food is taken into her stomach and it is there changed into liquid and so prepared, that when it passes into the intestines, the part of the food that is good for her, is sucked up into the blood, and the blood carries it to every part of her body. It distributes whatever is needed to all parts, and as the baby is a part, it gets its share. The other pipe carries the blood back again, out of the baby for new supplies, and as this is going on all the time, there is no danger of the baby starving in any way, or at any time.

When your daughter understands this, show her how important it is that mothers should be in good health, otherwise the baby will not get good food, it will not be properly nourished and will be born a poor, little sickly child. Little girls, consequently, should try to eat properly, exercise regularly, and do everything their mothers tell them, so that when they become mothers, they will be able to nourish their babies and not bring into the world poor little starved infants.

Girls Must not Become Mothers.—We have previously stated that girls can become mothers when they have reached the age of puberty. God did not intend, however, that girls at the age of twelve or fourteen should become mothers, because their bodies are not strong enough, nor are they fully grown, nor have they the experience, to undertake the physical task and responsibility of bringing a baby into the world. We know this from experience, because we have seen the sickly babies such girls have, and we have seen how much these girl mothers suffer, and how they ruin their health, by trying to do what God did not intend they should do.[Pg 185] Even the trees teach us this lesson. An orange tree will bring out buds, which would develop into oranges, when it is two years old. The experienced farmer, however, will pluck these buds off, and will do so every year, till the tree is five years old. If he allowed the tree to bear fruit during its young years, the oranges would not be good, or sweet, or large; so he waits until the tree has grown and is strong and healthy, when its fruit will be large and sweet. An orange tree of this type will have better fruit, and will continue to produce this good variety for many years. A tree allowed to bear fruit when two years old will never have first class oranges, nor will it continue to have, even poor oranges, as long as the other.

[Pg 187]

CHAPTER XV

PREPARING FOR MOTHERHOOD

Menstruation—Irregular Menstruation—Changes in the Quantity of the Flow—How the Womb is Held in Place—Symptoms of Menstruation—Menstruation Should Not be Accompanied with Pain—Don't Give Your Daughters Patent Medicines or "Female Regulators"—Take Your Daughter to the Doctor—Leucorrhea in Girls—Bathing when Menstruating—Constipation and Displaced Wombs—Dress and Menstruation—Absence of Menstruation, or Amenorrhea—Treatment of Amenorrhea—Painful Menstruation, or Dysmenorrhea—Causes of Dysmenorrhea—Treatment of Dysmenorrhea—Sterility in the Female—Conditions Which Affect the Fertility of Women—Climate—Station in Life—Season of the Year—Age—The Tendency to Miscarry—Causes of Sterility in the Female—Displacement of Womb—Diseases of Womb, Ovaries, or Tubes—Malformations—Lacerations—Tumors—Leucorrhea—Physical Debility—Obesity—Special Poisons—"Knack of Miscarrying"—Miscarriage—Cause of Miscarriage—The Course and Symptoms of Miscarriage—What to do when a Miscarriage is Threatened—Treatment of Threatened Miscarriage—Treatment of Inevitable Miscarriage—After Treatment of Miscarriage—The Tendency to Miscarriage.

MENSTRUATION

We have explained in the previous chapter what menstruation is, its frequency, its significance and its origin. There are a number of its common characteristics with which the mother and daughter should be acquainted.

Irregular Menstruation.—Menstruation may occur once (the first time) and fail to recur the following month or for a number of months. This need cause no alarm as long as the general health remains good. It will come again in its own time. Nervousness may cause a suspension of menstruation. This is quite common in school girls who are driven too hard at school, whose[Pg 188] sleep is interfered with, whose appetite is poor and who are allowed too many social indiscretions, as parties, dances, etc., where late hours are observed, all of which should be put aside until school life is over. Sometimes menstruation will temporarily stop if the girl goes away from home on a visit.

Sometimes the quantity will be greater than at other times, and a very scant flow, after it has been free and regular may cause apprehension. Various causes may be responsible for a decrease, catching cold, sitting on cold steps or cold ground, wearing damp clothes, nervousness, mental worry, physical exhaustion, insufficient food and exercise, and anemia, may cause it. For these reasons a girl should be exceedingly careful of her health, she should guard against catching cold. Do not change the underwear until certain that the weather is far enough advanced in season to justify such a change. She should not become exhausted or worry. In all cases of suppression, or of increased flow, a physician should be consulted at once, and girls should be instructed to tell their mothers of any change in the character of the "periods," as soon as it occurs. Mothers should instruct their daughters to rest the first day of their monthly flow, and all during the menstruation they should refrain from any unusual activity. Even play should be moderated and abstained from entirely if there is any pain. In order that the girl fully appreciates why these rules are laid down, it is advisable to explain just how the womb is held in place in her body.

This appears to the writer as being a particular important point. A girl must not be expected to give these matters the serious consideration they merit unless she thoroughly understands the reasons why. An explanation, in the form of even an intelligent talk, will soon be forgotten. If, however, a definite, concrete picture, is impressed upon her; if she actually sees in her mind the process that is going on, she will understand why it is necessary to do as she is told. If the mother will therefore assure herself that the daughter actually knows what is being accomplished in her womb at the menstrual period, she will carry out the instructions more faithfully.[Pg 189]

How the Womb is Held in Place.—The human uterus, or womb, is held in its proper place in much the same way as a clothes pin sits on a clothes line. The heavier part is the upper part, and that part is held in place partly by resting on the rectum behind, and the bladder in front. When menstruation occurs, the body of the womb becomes much heavier because of the increased amount of blood in its interior. This added weight increases its liability to tip over, and if any extra strain or effort is made at this time it will become tipped, or as the physician calls it, displaced. If a womb becomes displaced, every menstruation afterward will be painful and prolonged,—sometimes excessively so. A displaced womb becomes congested and unhealthy. It causes leucorrhea or a chronic discharge, makes a nervous wreck of the woman, results in sterility and frequently in a dangerous operation. There are, therefore, ample reasons for watchfulness and care on the part of the growing girl.

Symptoms of Menstruation.—After menstruation is established there should be no actual pain at each period. There are, however, certain undefined feelings,—premonitory symptoms,—which may be explained in the following terms:—A day or two before the date on which the menstruation is expected, the girl will appreciate that "her sickness" is coming. She will not, or should not, complain of pain, but will state that she has a bearing down feeling, is a little more nervous than usual, has no desire to go into company, and wants to be more or less her own entertainer. The "sick" period usually lasts four or five days. The second day is the most important.

Menstruation Should Not be Accompanied With Pain.—If any actual pain accompanies menstruation, either before or after it is established, the mother should at once take the daughter to the family physician. Menstruation is a natural, physiological act and should not be accompanied with actual distress or pain. It is astonishing how many mothers will allow their daughters to suffer needlessly, for months and years, because of the mistaken idea that "since the pain is there, it must be," or because she—the mother—suffered, so also must the[Pg 190] daughter suffer. There is no more unfortunate mistake, and many a girl's health and happiness has been blasted because of this misbelief. The cause of the pain is, in a vast majority of the cases, a very simple one, and can be removed in a very brief time.

Should the menstrual period last too long, be too frequent, or be in any way not what it should be, consult your physician. If you are not sure of "what it should be," or if you have any doubt, ask your doctor. Don't let any false pride or feeling of modesty on your part, or on the part of your daughter, dictate your policy under such circumstances. Don't take the advice of your friends or neighbors in a matter so vital. It is too important, and they are not qualified to "guess" any more than you are. Don't, if you have any respect for yourself, or love for your child, begin dosing her with the advertised patent medicines and "Female Regulators" for which so much is claimed, and which seem to "just suit" your daughter's case at this particular time. Take her to the doctor, whose advice you value (or you should not have him as a family physician), who has no interest at stake except to help you and your child, and whose fee is no more than the price of one of these bottles of advertised poison. He is the only one qualified to speak with authority on such a momentous subject, and you will never spend a dollar to better advantage. Warn your daughter not to speak about "her sickness" to other girls.

Especial attention should be paid to cleanliness during this period. The mistaken idea that bathing of any kind at this time may have disastrous consequences is responsible for much of this neglect. If proper care is taken warm sponge baths, in a warm room, will not cause any trouble. Unpleasant odors can be avoided by sponging the parts with a warm solution, into which a mild antiseptic is put, upon changing the cloths.

Leucorrhea in Girls.—It has been stated above that a displaced womb may cause leucorrhea or a discharge. It must be remembered that leucorrhea, or "whites," may occur in girls as well as in married women. It can also result from catching cold during the menstrual period. Another mistaken idea is that girls should not take[Pg 191] douches for fear of injuring the hymen. This is erroneous, and while they are entirely unnecessary in a vast majority of cases it is sometimes absolutely essential to douche in order to cure leucorrhea. When they are given, it is advisable to use the small nozzle that comes with every douche bag set.

Constipation and Displaced Wombs.—When the picture is fresh in the mind of the girl, of how the womb is held upright in her body, the mother should speak to her about the serious results that may occur from constipation. If the rectum is full of hardened feces the womb will be pushed out of place, and if under these circumstances straining is necessary to empty the bowel, and if this condition is habitual, constipation may be the actual cause of displacement of the womb.

Dress and Menstruation.—It is also an opportune time to demonstrate to what extent serious results may follow mistakes in dressing. The habit of permitting growing girls to constrict the waist, to bind and pull the abdomen by too tight garters, or too tight corset, is wrong, and no mother should permit it. In another part of the book, this matter is taken up more fully, but if it is explained to the girl while she is considering the subject of menstruation, she may more quickly and more fully appreciate its significance.

Absence of Menstruation—Amenorrhea.—The absence of menstruation after it has been established, does not, as a rule, indicate any disease of the womb or female sexual organs. It is to be regarded merely as a symptom and can be, as previously stated, safely ignored if the general health is good. If the general condition is poor, and the quantity and quality of the blood deficient, it is a provision of nature to suppress menstruation in the interest of the general health. For this reason it is safe to disregard the amenorrhea and build up the bodily strength. This explains why some girls pass the usual age of puberty and show no signs of menstruating. They are poorly developed sexually, through deficiency of blood. If, on the other hand, a girl should have all the symptoms of menstruation every month, but no flow, she should be examined by a physician to determine if there is any[Pg 192] obstruction to the escape of blood. Total absence of any symptoms of menstruation extending into adult life, may indicate an absence of the sexual organs. During the first year after puberty it is quite natural for menstruation to be irregular; after the function is thoroughly established there are many causes that may be responsible for its temporary absence.

Causes of Amenorrhea.—Any condition or circumstance which reduces the general health or impoverishes the quality or quantity of the blood and weakens the nervous system, will result in a stoppage of the monthly periods. Among these are insufficient food and exercise, overwork, overstudy, exposure to cold, sitting on cold steps or gold ground, wearing damp clothes, bathing in cold water at the beginning of menstruation, powerful emotions, as great fright, anger, anxiety; acute diseases, such as typhoid fever, cholera, the infectious skin diseases; chronic diseases such as Bright's disease, heart disease, consumption; anemia and chlorosis are very common causes. Obesity or an overfat condition will cause an early suppression of the menses which may result in a fruitless marriage. Displacement of the womb and other local disorders frequently result in scanty or delayed menstruation. Anxiety lest pregnancy may occur in the newly married may cause a delay in the periods. A radical change of climate or sometimes a visit to the country, or changed circumstances may stop the flow for the time being.

Treatment.—The treatment of amenorrhea, or absence of menstruation, will depend on the underlying cause. A careful investigation should be made into the mode of life and the hygienic surroundings of the patient. Her general health and her mental condition should be inquired into. If the patient is not in good health, or is not obtaining exercise in the open air, or if she is a victim of mental worry or of domestic unhappiness, or if any sufficient cause exists for the amenorrhea it must be removed before any treatment may be expected to relieve the condition. If the patient is a married woman the possibility of pregnancy should always be borne in mind, and no radical treatment instituted until this has[Pg 193] been excluded. If the absence of menstruation is dependent upon defective development of the sexual organs we cannot expect much from any treatment. The amenorrhea from exhaustive diseases will usually correct itself with, or soon after, the establishment of convalescence. In diseases which tend to death, as in consumption, heart disease, etc., the function is never reestablished. A very common habit of most people is to regard the absence of the monthly periods as the cause of their ill health. It is not, it is the result of the ill health. Get rid of the bad health and the menses will take care of themselves. That form of amenorrhea which is the result of change of climate or surroundings will regulate itself as soon as the victim becomes acclimated or reconciled to the change, or returns home if the visit is of brief duration.

As a general routine treatment, good wholesome food, regular hours, fresh air, sunlight, and judicious exercise, with such other measures as may be suggested by the condition of the blood and nervous system, are the indications in the way of treatment.

Anemia and chlorosis (poor blood) should be treated by the administration of iron in some form. Obesity should be reduced by diet, exercise, and such other treatment as may be found efficient and not detrimental to health. Overwork, mental and physical, should be stopped, and sedentary habits changed to a more active out-door life. The acute suppression from exposure to cold, wearing of damp clothes, sitting on cold stones or cold or damp ground, sea bathing in very cold water, is very often associated with an acute inflammation of the womb itself and calls for rest in bed, laxatives to open the bowel, hot application to the lower part of the abdomen and a teaspoonful of Hayden's Viburnum in a glass of hot water every four hours until relieved. The use of the sitz bath is frequently successful if taken at night followed by a laxative and a hot drink.

Painful Menstruation—Dysmenorrhea.—Most, if not all, victims of painful menstruation are of a nervous temperament. Dysmenorrhea is simply one symptom of the general nervous condition. The nervousness may be acquired or it may be the result of heredity. In girls it has been found to be an accompaniment of the overwork[Pg 194] and worry of school and student life. Girls who suffer greatly from it while in school are entirely free during vacation from school.

There is a type of painful menstruation known as neuralgic dysmenorrhea. This is simply a local expression of a general neuralgic tendency. It comes under conditions which favor neuralgias in other parts of the body. Girls and women affected with this type of dysmenorrhea are often anemic, hysterical, and not infrequently the victims of malaria, rheumatism, or other diseases which tend to impoverish the blood and reduce nerve vitality. The pain resembles neuralgia elsewhere. It comes and goes, it may last a brief time or a long time, it may be very mild or very severe. The pain bears no fixed relation to the flow, it may proceed, accompany or follow it.

Mechanical dysmenorrhea is that form in which a mechanical impediment exists to the escape of the menstrual fluid. The internal canal may be too small, displacement, growths, either inside or out of the womb, faulty development, or frequently simple congestion will act as an obstruction and cause pain from tension. The pain accompanying mechanical dysmenorrhea is very different from the neuralgic type. It comes on gradually, increases slowly until it is very severe and stops suddenly. A gush of blood from the womb announces the fact that the obstruction has been overcome and the womb has emptied itself; as soon as this occurs the pain ceases.

In the mechanical variety there are frequently clots in the menstrual flow. Inasmuch as this type may be caused by imperfect development of the womb, it is common to find that pain has characterized the monthly periods from the time of the first menstruation. It may, however, as stated above, be caused by growths which had their beginning at a later period.

Treatment.—For the neuralgic variety the treatment should be general. The whole object is to build up the general health. Fresh air, sunlight, out-door exercise, plain, substantial food, regular hours, pleasant surroundings, and such medication as may be indicated, should be[Pg 195] the course to follow. The bowels should be kept regular and digestion aided in every way possible, if necessary by rest from school, or work, or by a change of air and scene. If the patient is inclined to malaria she must take quinine and live in a locality free from that tendency. If rheumatic she should take the remedies advised in that disease and avoid colds, wet clothes, or sitting in cold, badly ventilated rooms, churches or theatres. If there are no distinct evidences of special tendencies, general tonics may be given to advantage. These should consist chiefly of iron, arsenic, phosphous, nux vomica, cod liver oil, etc.

The treatment of mechanical dysmenorrhea of course implies removal of the cause. As this necessitates operative procedure, or at least an examination by a physician, it is best left in his hands.

STERILITY

Sterility means the inability to become a parent. A woman who is sterile cannot become a mother. She is for some reason unable to have a baby.

A childless union is frequently the cause of much unhappiness. There is something lacking in the expression "a childless home." It seems a paradox, as home is inherently associated with children and happiness. It has been stated that one out of every eight marriages is barren. The average time which elapses after marriage and the birth of the first child is seventeen months. Physicians agree that if a woman goes over three years after marriage without having a baby her chances of having one are small. If children are desired, and they usually are by childless parents, every effort should be made within the first three years to ascertain the cause of the sterility, and if it can be rectified. The barrenness may be dependent upon some physical defect which will quickly respond to the proper medical treatment. It is well to remember, however, that the defect is not always the woman's. In every six childless marriages about one is due to sterility in the husband. The age of the greatest fertility in women is between twenty and twenty-four[Pg 196] years. It is rare to find a barren woman between these years. Nature evidently intended that the duties of maternity should be assumed between the twenty and twenty-fourth year. If married before the age of twenty the statistics prove that barrenness exists in one woman in every twelve. If married after the twenty-fourth year the chances of having children decreases with the age of the woman.

If a mother goes for three consecutive years without becoming pregnant the chances are that she will have no more children. Consequently if other children are desired it is unsafe to rest upon the assumption that a woman will again be a mother simply because she has been one in the past. Many conditions could, and may, have occurred since the last pregnancy (and may be as a result of that pregnancy) to change her natural fertility into a condition of temporary sterility. An examination should therefore be made before too long an interval elapses and the facts learned. It will usually be found in such cases that a displacement or laceration, or at most, some cause easily remedied is immediately responsible for the apparent barrenness.

CONDITIONS WHICH AFFECT THE FERTILITY OF WOMEN

Climate.—It is a well-known fact that more children are born in southern regions than in northern countries. It may be asserted, therefore, that climate affects the fertility of the race.

Station in Life.—Children are more numerous among the poor than among those who are wealthy and enjoy the luxury of riches. This condition cannot, however, be construed as a true expression of fertile efficiency. It is more a comparison of ethics, and when we express it thus we are giving it its most charitable name.

Season of the Year.—The spring of the year, being more favorable to fecundity, exerts an influence over the increase of population. Nursing mothers are as a rule sterile until after weaning time. This is not always so however, and the possibility of pregnancy taking place[Pg 197] while nursing a baby, and before menstruation is reestablished must be reckoned with as it occurs quite frequently.

Age.—Age may be said to affect the fertility of women inasmuch as sterility is the natural and proper condition before menstruation is established and after menstruation ceases.

The Tendency to Miscarry.—Because a woman has never given birth to a living child is no proof that she is sterile. Many women have the ability to conceive but for some reason they have acquired the misfortune, or the "knack," of miscarrying. This is a condition of the gravest significance and will be considered at length in its proper place.

The influence of a temporary separation has had excellent results in a great many historical cases. Where the married couple seem to be lacking in some one or other of the emotional or temperamental qualifications, it is advisable to suggest a temporary separation. When this period has expired and they resume marital relationship the element of novelty, acting as a stimulus, quite frequently reestablishes a fertility that was seemingly suspended, or awakens it if conception has never previously taken place.

There are a great many cases on record where, conditions having remained the same, women have become fertile after years of seeming barrenness. It is impossible to explain, or to satisfactorily understand these cases. It is quite common to note cases in which women have never become pregnant until a number of years after marriage, even when the desire to have children existed. There is one case on record of a woman married at eighteen, but although both herself and her husband enjoyed habitual good health, conception did not take place until she was forty-eight years of age when she bore a healthy child. Women should not, therefore, become easily discouraged in the hope of having a baby, especially when they have a clean history, and a healthy body. The conditions may change and may become favorable when hope is about to die.[Pg 198]

CAUSES OF STERILITY IN WOMEN

Inasmuch as it is necessary to consult a competent physician in all cases of sterility, it is not necessary to go into detail regarding each possible cause, other than to explain how each may produce barrenness. It will be observed that a competent physician is specified and advised in these cases. This is very important because many advertising, or "quack" doctors, particularly solicit these kind of cases. They are not competent to be trusted with such cases and will likely effect more harm than good. A woman should not hesitate to consult the best available medical authority if she is a victim of sterility. There is nothing to be ashamed of. It is a perfectly proper medical situation and should receive the best medical advice and investigation. The following are the more frequent causes of absolute sterility.

(A) Displacement of womb.

(B) Diseases of womb, ovaries or fallopian tubes.

(C) Malformations.

(D) Lacerations or tears of mouth of womb.

(E) Tumor.

(F) Leucorrhea.

(G) Physical debility.

(H) Special blood poisons.

(I) Great obesity.

(J) Anemia.

(K) Self-abuse.

(L) Habitual alcoholism.

(M) Lack of moderation in the marital relations.

(N) Certain diseases may be associated with barrenness: cancer, diabetes, consumption, Bright's disease, etc.

(O) Certain temperamental conditions may be associated with barrenness: lack of affinity, frigidity.

THE KNACK OF MISCARRYING

Displacement of Womb.—In many instances the primary cause of the displaced womb was some energetic, muscular effort, made while the victim was yet a girl,—probably before menstruation began. Whatever act first[Pg 199] caused a slight tilting of the womb, must necessarily have been an unusual physical effort, and as girls are getting more and more strenuous we may look for more trouble in this direction in the future. Inasmuch as a slight tilting of the womb gradually gets worse it is a reasonable expectation to believe that sterility is a natural sequence to displacement. The girl may have been the victim of painful menstruation which was neglected, because not quite painful enough to compel medical relief, which is sought for only as a last resource unfortunately under the circumstances. Intercourse may also have been more or less painful,—a condition which again is mistakenly and imprudently borne in silence and left to take care of itself. But when persistent sterility faces her, the woman seeks medical assistance and her trouble is discovered. As the displacement is found to be the cause of her sterility, its correction, which is a comparatively easy medical problem, not only cures the barrenness but happily relieves her of the menstrual distress and all other pain.

The treatment for displacement consist of placing medicated pieces of wool or cotton, called tampons, in the vagina in such a position as to hold the womb, *as* nearly in its proper place as is possible. After a time nature will so strengthen the ligaments that they will hold the womb and a cure is, therefore, affected. The length of time necessary to cure depends upon the length of time the displacement has existed. It may take, from two to four months. When the displacement is of long standing and is accompanied with more or less inflammation, adhesions sometimes grow between the womb and the adjacent organs. It is necessary to resort to surgery in such cases, but the result is always good and the danger practically nothing.

Disease of the Womb, Ovaries or Fallopian Tubes.—Disease of the womb, ovaries, and fallopian tubes, which renders the victim sterile, is as a rule the direct result of infection. Such infection is conveyed by the husband to the wife. This is quite a common condition. The simple fact that such conditions exist leads us to hope that the time is not far distant when it will be compulsory[Pg 200] for all participants in the marriage ceremony to submit to a thorough physical examination. By this means, and by this means only, will the innocent be protected. No one can conceive, unless he has been identified, as a physician, with one of the large metropolitan hospital clinics, of the extent of this class of disease, and of the frightful suffering caused, and innocent lives ruined, by infection conveyed in this way. It is a tragic corollary to the marriage vow "for better or for worse."

If a woman is fortunate enough to fall into the hands of an honorable physician, who will tactfully explain to her the serious significance of her condition and obtain her consent to treat her until she is cured, which in all probability will include a surgical operation, and will do so with diligence, without regard to the size of the bill, she will indeed be a lucky woman. It is from women who are suffering with such diseases,—most of them without the slightest idea of what ails them,—that the venders of advertised nostrums reap their fortunes, and it is from the same victims that most of the advertised medical "quacks" look for their blood-money. The great difficulty, however, lies in the failure of the woman to appreciate the seriousness of her condition, and as a consequence she fails to understands why it should take so long to cure her. She loses confidence in her physician, she buys certain "cures" recommended to her by Mrs. Busybody and later tries other physicians and ends by losing faith in herself. Meantime she grows worse and worse. There are thousands such. It may be here stated without fear of contradiction that if the public in general would repose more confidence in the medical profession, there would be much less suffering, much less sorrow, fewer regrets, fewer irresponsible "isms," and cults, because there would be fewer disappointed individuals to support them. If the medical profession would condescend to employ the tactics and devices of those questionable, fashionable agencies that claim the power to cure human suffering, it could quickly reap the profit and the laudation that it now escapes because it keeps the faith.

The way to be cured of any disease, if it is curable,[Pg 201] is to engage a reputable physician and follow his instructions implicitly. Let him understand you expect him to see you through your trouble and let him know you have confidence in him. There isn't one physician in a thousand who will cheat you under these circumstances.

Malformation.—Under this heading are all those cases of sterility resulting from imperfect generative organs. These are products of a failure on the part of nature to furnish or develop the structures participating in the propagation of the species. The entire generative organs are sometimes wanting. The womb may have failed for some reason to grow with the rest of the body, it remains (as it is known) as an "infantile womb." Occasionally the womb grows together, that is, it is solid instead of being a hollow organ. The mouth of the womb may be too small, representing what is called "a pin head opening." The natural opening is large enough to admit a lead pencil, a "pin head opening" would not be larger than the lead in the pencil. The latter condition is quite a common cause of sterility and is readily amenable to treatment. Most of the malformations which produce sterility are impossible to cure.

Lacerations or Tears in Mouth of Womb.—This subject is fully discussed on another page of this volume.

Tumor.—A tumor may be so situated as to prevent conception, or it may involve the body of the womb constituting a reason in itself for sterility.

Leucorrhea.—Leucorrhea or "the whites" may be of such an acid character as to kill the spermatozoa in the vagina, or it may be of such volume as to render impregnation impossible. The treatment of this condition is discussed elsewhere.

Physical Debility.—When the general health is bad, no matter from what cause, sterility usually exists. This lack of vitality may be due to chronic disease, or it may have been caused by a very severe acute illness, such as typhoid fever. One's mode of living, if unhygienic, may be responsible for continued bad health and a consequent sterility.

Obesity.—Very fat women are usually barren. If a[Pg 202] woman rapidly accumulates fat after marriage she as a rule does not have more than one or two children. Women often become stout immediately after the child bearing age ceases.

Special Poisons.—Certain special poisons in the blood cause sterility by producing miscarriage.

MISCARRIAGE

By the term "miscarriage" we mean that for some reason the progress of pregnancy has been interrupted and the fetus is expelled from the womb. A miscarriage or abortion (both terms meaning the same—the difference between the two terms is a technical one and need not concern us here) can occur any time after conception up to approximately the seventh month, when, if labor takes place, the child may be born alive. The condition would then be termed a premature labor. A miscarriage or abortion is an immature labor and implies an immature or dead child.

The condition is a serious one no matter whether it is attended with grave symptoms or apparently no symptoms. If it occurs shortly after conception, during the first few months of married life it is serious, if not in its physical consequences, it is in its significance, because it establishes the tendency to miscarry,—a tendency that may result in great mental distress because of the worry and fear it engenders, and of sorrow and heartache because it may blast the hope of parentage. Such a miscarriage may take place at once after conception. If so, the following menstruation may be delayed for a week or so and is then a little more profuse than is customary. This will be the only indication that a life has been sacrificed that the young wife may have, and frequently the significance of such an occurrence is never understood, yet the tendency to miscarry is nevertheless established, and a seeming sterility is apparently the fate of the woman. It is, therefore, of the greatest importance that extreme care should be taken to bring the first pregnancy to a successful consummation. A young wife should realize that she is apt to become pregnant at[Pg 203] any time. Her conduct therefore should be such at least as not to harm the life principle with which she has been entrusted. To this end any excessive sexual activity should be strictly avoided.

Causes of Miscarriage.—Any strenuous physical effort must be guarded against. Included in such efforts may be the following: dancing, running, jumping, surf-bathing, sewing on a machine, sweeping, washing, house-cleaning, moving furniture, etc. Sometimes the primary cause of a miscarriage is to be found in some hygienic act, such as a hot bath, too prolonged or too many hot douches near the menstrual periods. A blow or a fall, even a fright or shock may cause a miscarriage. Anything that violently shakes or agitates the womb, which may at this time be irritable because of its condition, will be sufficient to excite it to contract and miscarry. Hence violent coughing or vomiting should be avoided if possible; horseback riding, jolting in a carriage, convulsions, hysterical crying, may also be the causative factors. Displacement of the womb by limiting its tendency to grow when pregnant, may cause it to miscarry. Very severe general diseases such as small-pox, pneumonia, etc., will cause the womb to empty itself. Disease of the fetus or the presence of syphilis in either of the parents will also have the same result.

The Course and Symptoms of Miscarriage.—The cause of a miscarriage or abortion is much the same as an ordinary labor at term. Whatever interrupts the pregnancy causes the death of the fetus. The dead fetus acts as a foreign body and excites the womb to contract as it does during an ordinary confinement. The contractions open up the mouth of the womb and the fetus is expelled together with its membranes and after-birth. The significant and the most important symptom of a miscarriage or abortion is hemorrhage or bleeding from the privates. The flow of blood may not amount to much or it may be excessive and alarming; it may not be constant, it may come from time to time in the form of clots.

The next significant and important symptom of miscarriage or abortion is pain. The pain, like the flow of[Pg 204] blood, may be only slight or it may be very severe, sometimes it is absent in very early miscarriage. As a rule the pain is severe when the miscarriage occurs after pregnancy has lasted for a number of months.

A miscarriage or abortion is said to be "complete" when the fetus with its membranes and after-birth is expelled clean and whole, or in other words when the womb empties itself completely. A miscarriage or abortion is said to be "incomplete" when some part of the embryo is left in the womb.

What to Do When a Miscarriage is Threatened.—When a woman, who is pregnant, begins to flow she should at once go to bed and keep perfectly quiet and send for a physician. A miscarriage is a treacherous condition and is so regarded by all medical men. It may not amount to much or it may, on the other hand, develop into a serious situation. The immediate danger is from hemorrhage; the ultimate or remote danger is sepsis or blood poisoning. The condition is one that can only be taken in charge by a qualified physician in whose hands we can safely leave the conduct of the case.

As a general rule it is quite safe to assert that a woman will not bleed enough at the beginning of a miscarriage to do any permanent harm. Consequently there is no occasion for unnecessary alarm. She must, however, as stated above, heed the warning and go to bed, keep perfectly quiet and send for a physician. If she fails to follow this advice it is quite possible that she may have a hemorrhage during the course of the miscarriage of a sufficiently serious character to endanger her life or from the effects of which she may suffer for the remainder of her life.

There is practically no danger during the course of or after a "complete" miscarriage. The danger which may ensue from an "incomplete" miscarriage is hemorrhage and a form of poisoning caused by the absorption into the system of putrifying products of the part of the dead embryo left in the womb.

There are a large number of cases of criminal abortion in which septic poisoning occurs caused by the[Pg 205] utensils or instruments used in inducing the abortion. All of these cases are operative cases which must be attended to promptly to save life.

Treatment of Threatened Miscarriage.—Not all of the cases of beginning miscarriage end in miscarriage. If the physician is sent for in time he can very frequently give directions that will, if carried out faithfully, avert the disaster. Success is more likely to attend those cases in which the trouble has been caused by some accidental injury, as a fall, or blow, or extra exertion. This is more especially the case if the woman has previously borne children, is healthy and in good condition and whose womb is known not to be diseased. In these cases there is a partial separation of the fetus from the wall of the womb, which causes the bleeding. The physician will direct that the woman be put to bed, in a quiet, darkened room. He will instruct the nurse to sterilize the external genital region: a sterile gauze dressing is then left in place. Some form of prescription will be given to diminish the patient's nervous fear and to allay any tendency on the part of the womb to contract. It is always essential and very important to save everything that passes from the womb during the course of a threatened miscarriage in order that the physician may know exactly just what the condition is. Each cloth, each clot of blood will have to be examined before the proper treatment can be pursued in safety.

When the miscarriage cannot be prevented it is called an "Inevitable miscarriage."

Treatment of an Inevitable Miscarriage.—In these cases every precaution is taken, just as in a normal confinement, to avert blood poisoning. The hands, instruments, dressings, etc., are carefully rendered sterile and the whole field must be surgically clean. The physician will conduct the case as conditions justify and as the situation develops.

After Treatment of a Miscarriage.—It is one of the many thankless tasks of a physician's life to insist on each patient staying in bed at least ten days after a miscarriage. The average woman and frequently the intelligent woman fails to appreciate the absolute necessity[Pg 206] for this procedure. It is necessary and it is the physician's duty to insist on it being done in the interest of the woman. Many of the multitude of diseases of women are caused by disregarding advice on such occasions.

The Tendency to Miscarry.—If a woman, for any reason, has had a miscarriage, her womb will tend to miscarry at the same period during a subsequent pregnancy. If the miscarriage should occur during her first pregnancy the tendency to miscarry will be greater than if acquired after she has had a baby.

This is one of the reasons why young wives often fail to have children. They "get rid" of the first one or two, because they are not ready to have children, or because they want some enjoyment themselves before they are tied down with a family. Having established the habit their womb has been educated to abort, and it will keep this habit up, much to their astonishment and chagrin.

Young wives should therefore faithfully follow out all the rules of the Hygiene of Pregnancy laid down by their physician, and which are given in detail in this book.[Pg 207]

Courtesy of New York World At Work with the Calipers

Watching carefully the physical development of the child month by month is one of those many little things which may result in disaster if neglected.

Abnormal development, or lack of development, should be promptly reported to the physician, as it may be a warning of serious trouble.

For the table of standards, mental and physical, adopted by the American Medical Society see page 271.

[Pg 208]

THE BABY

[Pg 209]

CHAPTER XVI

HYGIENE AND DEVELOPMENT OF THE BABY

What to Prepare for the Coming Baby—Care of the Newly-born Baby—The First Bath—Dressing the Cord—Treatment After the Cord Falls off—A Pouting Navel—Bathing Baby—Clothing the Baby—Baby's Night Clothes—Care of the Eyes—Care of the Mouth and First Teeth—Care of the Skin—Care of the Genital Organs—Amusing Baby—Temperature in Children—The Teeth—The Permanent Teeth—Care of the Teeth—Dentition— Treatment of Teething—How to Weigh the Baby—Average Weight of a Male Baby—Average Weight of a Female Baby— Average Height of a Male Child—The Rate of Growth of a Child—Pulse Rate in Children—Infant Records, Why They Should be Kept—"Growing Pains."

What to Prepare For the Coming Baby.—The physician should instruct the young wife just what to provide for the coming baby. The following list will be found useful as a general guide.

An ordinary clothes basket, padded and lined, is quite sufficient for the first month; or, a baby crib, which may be cheap or expensive as the individual taste dictates. The Taylor crib is probably the handiest and best one on the market.

Pin cushion;

Puff-box and puff;

Soap box containing pure castile soap;

Hair brush and fine comb;

Two wash cloths;

Four ounces of crystal boracic acid, a saturated solution of which is used for cleansing baby's eyes and mouth;

One pound of good absorbent cotton;

A flexible tube of white vaseline;

A bath thermometer;

A package of sterile gauze;

A half dozen baby towels, good quality;

A soft, white, good blanket,—one and one-half yards square;

One pair small blunt pointed scissors;[Pg 210]

A package of the best safety pins;

Three or four dozen bird's-eye cotton diapers. First size, eighteen inches square. Second size, twenty-five inches square;

One yard of soft white flannel for belly bands; each band should be five inches wide, by twenty-four inches long.

Two silk and wool shirts;

Three flannel shirts (all shirts should be high necked, long sleeved, and open down the front);

Three Eiderdown wrappers;

Three Cashmere sacques;

Three pads for crib;

Six dresses;

Six petticoats (they should be thirty-three inches long from neck to hem; they should be turned up at the bottom for about four inches and should button there to keep the feet warm; if it is desired to use pinning blankets for the first two months in place of the petticoats, they should be made of soft white flannel with cotton bands);

Six night slips;

Six pair socks;

Two cloaks;

Two hoods;

One dozen bibs.

Simplicity, warmth, and freedom are the essentials in latter-day baby clothes. It is cheaper to make the clothes than to buy them. Excellent and accurate paper patterns can be obtained, giving the quantity of material necessary and suggesting the kind and quality best suited for the purpose. These patterns may be obtained from the Butterick Publishing Company in New York City.

Care of the Newly-Born Baby.—After the nurse has completed her duties with the mother after the confinement, she will prepare to give baby its first bath.

The bath should be given in a warm room. This is a matter that should receive more consideration than has been given it. Nurses do not as a rule attach much importance to this duty, while in reality it is a most important one. I have seen trained nurses make ready to give baby its first bath in rooms, during the night, that were not heated adequately. I am convinced that many babies have been victims of this careless habit to the extent of grafting on them the tendency to catarrhal colds and bronchitis because of undue exposure at this critical period. If one will remember that a baby has just been[Pg 211] removed from an environment where the temperature was suitable and constant, to one in which it needs a large degree of artificial heat until such time as it may become accustomed to the change, one may appreciate the risk taken in exposing the child for even a short time. The mother should therefore warn the nurse not to undertake the baby's first bath until the temperature and other conditions are favorable. Many nurses and other individuals have the impression, without knowing why, that the baby should be cleansed and bathed immediately after birth. This is not at all necessary. If the conditions are not favorable, it would be far better to wrap the baby snugly in a warm blanket—first having put a diaper on—and place it in its crib with a hot water bottle near it and defer the bathing until the following forenoon. By that time the baby will be adapted to its new surroundings; its lungs will have become accustomed to the air which it is breathing for the first time; the mother will have been rendered comfortable; in other words, the conditions and the environment will be favorable for the baby and for a better performance of the duty.

The next important feature of the first bath is that it should be done in the quickest time consistent with efficient service. Only the necessary exposure should be indulged in. It is not necessary that the baby should be exposed to the admiring inspection of every member of the household—there will be plenty of time for that without risking the health of the child. A pan of water at a temperature of 100° F. should be placed on a stool in front of the nurse. The nurse should have on a rubber apron, and on top of this, an ordinary apron and a warm bath towel laid over her knees. The child should be gently rubbed with warm sweet oil to remove the *vernix caseosa* (the greasy substance which is on all babies when born to a lesser or greater extent). Particular attention is to be given to all folds of the skin, as under the arms, in the fold of the neck, in the groin, behind the ears, etc., because in these parts the substance is thickest and if not carefully removed it will cake, and cause painful eruptions and sores, which may bleed and render the infant extremely uncomfortable. It is not necessary to[Pg 212] expose the whole body at one time while applying the oil. The lower half may be covered with a warm soft towel while the nurse is oiling the upper part, and vice versa. After the body has been thoroughly oiled it should be cleansed with water at the proper temperature, in which pure castile soap has been dissolved. Absorbent cotton only should be used to wash the baby. All the washing is done with the baby on the nurse's knee; it is not put into the water.

The baby should be mopped dry with sterile gauze, or with a soft sterile towel, the cord dressed and the flannel band adjusted. It should then be completely dressed and put to the nipple and later to sleep.

Dressing the Cord.—The cord should be covered with powder and sterile gauze. The powder to use should be plain subnitrate of bismuth. If there is any reason to use another powder the physician will write a prescription for it according to indications. The subnitrate of bismuth will be found much better than any ordinary talcum or toilet powder, many of which do not make good dressing powders.

Very few nurses know how to dress the cord. It seems to be impossible to impress them with the need of frequent attention to the cord. Fresh powder should be put on every time the diaper is removed, every time the infant urinates, and at other times during the day. The cord should be kept absolutely dry. Putting on powder twice daily will not keep the cord dry and many nurses are too lazy to bother to do it oftener. You cannot make a mistake in putting on too much powder, you can make a serious mistake by not putting on enough. Every time the cord is powdered it should be lifted up, away from the skin of the abdomen, and the powder put below it. The cord should be slightly drawn out and the powder applied round its base where it meets the skin. Many nurses are afraid to touch or handle the cord—they find it easier to neglect it. The mother should see that the nurse dresses the cord at least five times every day.

Applying the Sterile Gauze to the Cord.—A piece of gauze, six inches square is taken, a hole is cut the size of a ten-cent piece out of the center, the cord is drawn[Pg 213] through the hole, the gauze folded lengthwise over the cord and then sidewise, and this is held in place by the binder. This piece of gauze will adhere to the cord and will most likely be removed with the cord on the fifth day. If it should fall off, another piece may be put on in the same way.

If the cord does not fall off until very late it is because it has not been attended to rightly or because it was a very thick cord.

Treatment After the Cord Falls Off.—The stump of the cord should be powdered with the same powder used on the cord; a pad two inches square of sterile gauze and quite thick should be held over the stump for a number of days by the abdominal binder. This is used to prevent a possible rupture. After a week the size of the pad may be reduced, but a small pad should be used over the stump of the cord for a month or more.

A Pouting Navel.—If the stump of the cord should protrude, a piece of strong pasteboard, the size of a fifty-cent piece, should be wrapped in soft gauze and placed over the navel, over this a gauze pad, and if necessary this should be held in place by a strip of adhesive plaster, though the binder is usually sufficient if it is put on carefully. If this pad is held properly and worn for a month the tendency to protrusion or rupture will have passed away. These pads may of course, be removed when the baby is being bathed and put back again before the binder is applied.

Bathing Baby.—A baby should not be put into water for a bath until after the cord has been off for forty-eight hours.

During the first few months the temperature of the water should be 98° F. The temperature of the water should be taken with a bath thermometer; it should not be guessed at. A bath thermometer is an inexpensive commodity and it will be in daily use in many ways in a home where there is a baby—it should therefore be procured wherever possible. The room should be warm; there should be no draughts. The mother or nurse should cultivate the habit of bathing baby quickly and with system. Everything should be ready and at hand. A little[Pg 214] salt in the water will tend to strengthen the skin; it will also relieve any superficial rashes or excoriations which may be on the skin. Four tablespoonfuls to a gallon of water will be sufficient. The sea salt sold in the stores may be used in lesser quantities.

By the end of the fifth month the temperature of the water may be reduced to 95° F., and by the end of the first year to 90° F. After the first year the mother should accustom the child to a quick sponge with cool water on the chest and spine immediately after the bath. This simple means, if kept up, will often prevent the development of colds and bronchial troubles so common to children in temperate latitudes.

The best time to give the warm bath is at night. In the morning a cold sponge bath is desirable. This should be given as described in the chapter on cold sponge or shower baths.

In certain children bathing seems to depress their entire system. They do not react well even to a warm bath. They remain blue or pale around the mouth and eyes; bathing should therefore be carefully undertaken with these children until such time as they acquire strength.

Clothing of Baby.—The baby should wear a woolen shirt, with a high neck and long sleeves. The abdominal binder may be worn for the first three months. It is not necessary after that time. If worn longer the habit is acquired and chronic indigestion may ensue when it is ultimately taken off. If the baby is very thin it may be wise to leave it on, simply for its warming effect, for a few months longer. If the child is normal and healthy the binder should be left off permanently after three months. The band for the first four weeks should be made of plain flannel; after this period a knitted band with shoulder straps is the better article. All petticoats and skirts should be supported from the shoulders. Stockinet is a good material for diapers; it is soft, warm, and pliable.

Baby's feet should be warm always. Cold feet are frequently responsible for colic and gastro-intestinal troubles. A hot water bottle should be placed in the carriage if the weather is cold, but care should be taken[Pg 215] to see that it does not touch the feet, otherwise it may burn them. The same measure may be adopted in the baby's crib if the feet are cold.

During the summer the outer clothing should be made of the thinnest quality of material possible, and the underclothing of the finest flannel or gauze. Body heat may be maintained during changes of temperature by extra outer wraps—not by dressing the baby in clothes that keep it too hot and uncomfortable all the time.

The main object to be attained in clothing the baby is to ensure a sufficient protection, but the clothing must be light, warm, loose, and non-irritating. Don't bundle up the arms and legs so that they cannot be moved; don't pin them so tight that the child cannot breathe properly and don't put the band on so that the child is in torture all the time from inability to move the abdomen.

Baby's Night Clothes.—The night clothing should be the same as that worn during the day, but it should be loose and of the lightest flannel material. For older children a thin woolen shirt (not the one worn during the day) and a suit of union clothing with feet is best.

The mistake must not be made to cover children too warmly at night. They can do with relatively less than adults. Too much covering will render the sleep restless, will encourage nightmare, and in older children will engender bad habits. Delicate children especially must not be over-covered at night.

For the first few months children should sleep in a darkened room.

Care of the Eyes.—The eyes should be cleansed for the first few days with a saturated solution of boracic acid. They should be protected from the direct light for two or three weeks after birth.

Care of the Mouth and First Teeth.—Boiled cooled water should be used to cleanse the mouth every morning after the bath. A soft piece of sterile gauze should used for this purpose. The mother must guard against using too much force in cleaning the mouth of an infant.

The milk teeth should receive attention. If they are allowed to become dirty they will become carious and[Pg 216] cause bad breath and neuralgia. Teeth of this character are a menace to health because they harbor germs and in this way infect the mouth and cause stomach troubles. Teeth that are carious should be filled or removed.

Care of the Skin.—The skin of a baby, because of its delicate character, is susceptible to the slightest changes in the weather or to the condition of the digestive organs. Babies are frequently subject to rashes, intertrigo, excoriations, eczema, and other skin affections. It is much easier to prevent these conditions than to cure them. Cleanliness, not only in giving a daily efficient bath, but in every other respect, is essential. Castile soap only should be used, and no rubbing indulged in, simply mopping the parts with gauze well saturated with soapy water. All napkins should be removed as soon as soiled. If the skin is easily chafed the child should be bathed in salt water or water in which bran is mixed as explained in the chapter on bran baths.

The baby should be well powdered with a good quality of toilet powder. Ordinary starch, or talcum, or the stearate of zinc is suitable. Fat infants should be powdered in all the skin folds; otherwise they are sure to chafe.

Care of the Genital Organs.—The mother should make it a habit to remove any dirt from the genitals of the baby during the morning bath. Fecal matter sometimes gets into the folds of the female baby; this should be removed promptly. In older female children, dirt and dust get into the genitals which often has to be removed carefully with a soft piece of cloth. An exceedingly chronic form of inflammation is often seen in poor children because of neglect of these parts.

In male babies the mother must daily push back the foreskin and clean under it. If this is not done the natural secretion will gather there and cause much trouble. If the foreskin is long, the child should be circumcised; if it is not long it must be pushed back daily for a number of weeks; otherwise it will contract and it may be necessary to operate on it at a later date. If this is not faithfully attended to the prepuce will become adherent, the child becomes nervous and irritable, and it[Pg 217] may become addicted to self-abuse at a very early date—simply because the mother is derelict in the performance of her duty. If you are afraid to do your duty, don't neglect it, ask the doctor to show you just what has to be done and just how it should be done. You will find it to be a simple matter when you know how, as most things are.

Amusing Baby.—Mothers should understand that it is not necessary to amuse a baby under one year of age. Their nervous systems are not ready for any such sport. To excite a baby to laughter is to subject it to a shock which may injure it. The healthy development of the brain of a child demands quiet and restful surroundings. It should sleep, eat, and be allowed to amuse itself in a natural way.

Temperature in Children.—The normal temperature in a child varies more than it does in an adult. The rectal range may be between 98° and 99.5° F. and may be normal to that particular child. A rectal temperature of 97.5° F. or of 100.5° F. is of no importance unless it continues.

The best place to take the temperature in a child is the rectum and the next best place is in the groin. The temperature will always be from a half to a full degree higher in the rectum than in the groin. The thermometer should be left in the rectum for two minutes, and in the groin for five minutes.

The temperature in a child is a very fair guide as to the severity of the disease. It must be remembered, however, that a child will develop a temperature of two or three degrees from a very slight cause. It is not the height of the fever that is significant, but rather the duration of the fever that is important. A fever of 102° F. in a child may only mean a slight indigestion which will wholly disappear after a laxative is given, while the same degree of temperature in an adult usually means something much more serious. The degree of the temperature therefore should not occasion unnecessary worry; if, however, it continues and if the child shows other signs of illness, it may be regarded as indicating an abnormal condition which should be immediately found out. A temperature[Pg 218] of 100° F. to 102° F. usually means a mild illness, and one of 104° F. or over, a serious sickness.

It is not advisable that the ordinary mother should possess a clinical thermometer. There are many occasions when a child will have a fever which should not cause any worry; if the mother gets the thermometer habit, she will many times occasion unnecessary calls of the physician only to learn that they are false fears.

The Teeth.—There is no definite time at which the first teeth appear. They usually come between the sixth and eighth months. They may not, however, come until much later; or they may come earlier than the sixth month; and yet the child may be perfectly healthy. They come as a rule in the following order:

1. The two lower middle teeth,	6 to 8 months.
2. The four upper middle teeth,	8 to 10 months.

3. One on each side of two lower middle teeth, 8 to 12 months.

4. One on each side, above and below, back of above teeth (four in all), 12 to 15 months.

5. The next one on each side, above and below, back of those already in (four in all), 18 to 24 months.

6. The four back teeth on each side, above and below, 24 to 30 months.

At 1 year a child should have 6 teeth

At 1-1-2 years a child should have 12 teeth

At 2 years a child should have 16 teeth

At 2-1-2 years a child should have 20 teeth

They may not come in the above regular order even in well children. The upper front teeth may come first. If the child is sickly there may be marked irregularity in the order in which they appear. Twenty teeth comprise the first set.

The Permanent Teeth.—This set consists of thirty-two teeth. They begin about the sixth year and they are usually not complete until the twentieth year. They appear in the following order:[Pg 219]

First molars 6 years

Incisors 7 to 8 years

Bicuspids 9 to 10 years

Canines 12 to 14 years

Second molars 12 to 15 years

Third molars 17 to 25 years

Care of the Teeth.—The teeth should be given attention as soon as they appear. It is an excellent custom to wash the teeth and gums twice daily with a piece of clean absorbent cotton rolled round the finger of the mother and dipped in a saturated solution of boracic acid. This should be done up to the second year. After the second year a soft brush should be used and the teeth thoroughly cleaned morning and night with pure castile soap or a powder. The teeth of every child should be examined by a dentist every six months. All cavities should be filled with a soft filling. The milk teeth should not decay, but should fall out, or be forced out by the second set. A child should be taught to gargle early and a mouth wash should be used morning and night.

Dentition.—As a general rule the process of teething is accompanied by some symptoms. There may be fever, restlessness, and loss of appetite; though in many cases there are absolutely no symptoms. Some children seem to teethe hard, others easily. The same child may have some teeth without pain, and with others it may suffer severely. The condition of the child at the time, its age, and the season of the year undoubtedly have an influence. Children who are sickly and puny may have much difficulty while teething.

The degree of sickness varies quite considerably. There may only be, as stated above, slight fever, restlessness, with loss of appetite; or there may be, in addition to these symptoms, a pronounced fermentative diarrhea, which may lead to serious intestinal diseases; frequently there is a cough. This is more apt to be the case if the child is teething during the hot season.

Treatment.—When dentition affects the child's disposition it is a good plan to reduce the feeding in quantity and quality for the time being. If the child is bottle-fed,[Pg 220] two ounces can be taken out of each bottle and one ounce of boiled water added. If the child is breast-fed, he should be given two ounces of warm, boiled water before each feeding, and the actual feeding time at the breast shortened.

Rubbing the gum over the erupting tooth with a clean cloth may aid in helping it through. If the child is very restless and has lost sleep, the cloth may be moistened with brandy and water. Lancing the gum, though it is seldom done now-a-days, is justified in a few cases. Teething is not the cause of actual disease as was once thought, but it must be remembered that a child whose vitality is reduced by fever, restlessness, loss of appetite, loss of sleep, and irregular bowels, is more susceptible to disease than when enjoying robust health.

Sometimes a child will have a fever for one or two weeks during a hard dentition. There is apt to be more or less intestinal indigestion and fermentation at this time and as a consequence actual intestinal disease may develop. To avoid such a possibility it is an excellent plan to give an occasional dose of castor oil to clean thoroughly the whole intestinal canal. This should be done irrespective of the condition of the bowel, because frequently a diarrhea is caused by retained fermenting products.

Mothers must not acquire the habit of attributing all symptoms to the teething process simply because the child is teething. It must be remembered that a child may get a disease, or an ailment, while teething, that has nothing to do with teething. If this is neglected, serious consequences may result. Many children have lost their lives by a mother's carelessness in this way. Be on the safe side, consult your doctor; let him assume the responsibility.

How to Weigh the Baby.—The test of weight is one of the most satisfactory we possess as an indication of physical progress and health. It is not an absolute test, but it may safely be relied upon. The fattest baby is not necessarily the healthiest. A gradual and a uniform increase is a satisfactory growth. At birth a baby weighs, on an average, from seven to eight pounds, though some[Pg 221] babies weighing less are equally healthy. The normal and customary gain is from four to six ounces every week after birth.

The baby should be weighed about the same time of the day each week, and before a meal.

The average weight of a male child at different ages is as follows:

Birth	7-1/2 lbs.
3 weeks	8 lbs.
1 month	8-1/2 lbs.
3 months	12 lbs.
4 months	13-1/2 lbs.
5 months	15 lbs.
6 months	15-1/2 lbs.
7 months	17 lbs.
9 months	19 lbs.

1 year	21 lbs.
1-1/2 years	23 lbs.
2 years	26-1/2 lbs.
3 years	31-1/2 lbs.
4 years	35-1/2 lbs.
5 years	40 lbs.
6 years	45 lbs.
7 years	49 lbs.
8 years	54 lbs.
9 years	59 lbs.
10 years	65-1/2 lbs.

A female child weighs about one-fifteenth less than a male child, as a rule.

Table showing the average height of a male child, at different ages:

At birth	20-1/2 in.
6 months	26 in.
1 year	29 in.
2 years	32-1/2 in.
3 years	35 in.
4 years	38 in.
5 years	41-1/2 in.
6 years	44 in.
7 years	46 in.
8 years	48 in.
9 years	50 in.
10 years	52 in.

The Rate of Growth of a Child.—A child grows most rapidly during its first year—six to seven inches; from fourth to sixteenth, about two inches annually; thence to twentieth, one inch. Commonly, a child at two and a half years has attained half of its ultimate adult stature. The diseases of youth always accelerate growth.

Pulse Rate in Children and Adults.—Normal Pulse,—of new born, 130 to 140, per minute; first year, 105 to 115; second year, 106 to 115; third year, 95 to 105; fifth[Pg 222] to twelfth year, 80 to 90; thirteenth to twenty-first year, 75 to 80; twenty-first to sixtieth year, 70 to 75; in old age, 75 to 85.

Infant Records.—A record should be kept by the mother of every child which would embrace exact data as to weight, diet, size, development of mental power, teeth, ailments, sickness, pains, etc., with dates and any information which would aid in recalling exact conditions. Such records are of the utmost value in a number of ways. They help in giving suggestions as to diet, general health, and mental qualities of the child in question, and they aid in furnishing what physicians call "past history," which past history has a very valuable significance in estimating the character and importance of sickness during later years.

Such a record is also of importance in comparing a child's development with what is regarded as standard development, and also with the growth and development of other children in or out of the family.

If a child should thus be found to fall seriously below the standard and yet not appear actually sick, a very thorough and routine investigation should be instituted to discover if possible the cause. Some error might thus be detected which might seriously affect the child's future growth and well-being.

The date of the closing of the soft spot on the baby's head should be noted, and if it is still open, when it should be closed, it might mean that the child has a serious brain condition. The soft spot should close between the eighteenth and twenty-fourth months. The family physician should be notified if the soft spot is open later than the second year, as he may want to investigate the cause.

Should the child be unusually backward in walking, and when it does so should limp and feel pain in the knees, it should be examined for any symptom of hip joint disease, of which these are the earliest signs.

If the child complains of so-called "growing pains," keep in mind that these are rheumatic and may need attention. There are no such pains as actual "growing pains," that is, pains caused by the child growing.

[Pg 223]

CHAPTER XVII

BABY'S FEEDING HABITS

Overfeeding Baby—Intervals of Feeding—How Long Should a Baby Stay at the Breast—Vomiting Between Feedings—Regularity of Feeding—Why is Regularity of Feeding Important—"A Baby Never Vomits"—What is the Significance of So-called Vomiting After Feedings—Mothers Milk That is Unfit for Baby—Fresh Air for Baby—Air Baths for Baby.

Overfeeding Baby.—Every nursing mother should have printed and hung up, so she may read it every time she nurses her child, the following motto: "DON'T OVERFEED BABY." Few, if any, babies die of willful starvation: many die as a result of overfeeding. Mistaken kindness and lack of judgment are responsible for one-half of all the troubles of infancy. Babies require much less than is constantly given them. The stomach of a baby at birth will not hold more than one ounce, which is two tablespoonfuls; and at two months it will not hold more than three tablespoonfuls; and at six months, six or seven tablespoonfuls. Read these quantities once again carefully and try to realize the significance of the smallness of them. A baby is just like a little pig; it will go on feeding as long as it is allowed. The baby does not reason; it has no judgment; it depends upon its mother's judgment. If the mother is false to the trust the baby overloads its stomach. A swollen, distended, overloaded stomach causes indigestion. A baby with indigestion is a colicky, fretty, sick baby. Overfeeding, therefore, is the beginning of lots of trouble to the mother, and needless pain and suffering and sickness to the baby. A simple matter, but it is one of the most difficult lessons nursing mothers have to learn.

Overfeeding is most apt to occur at night. Many mothers put the child to the nipple for its regular feeding and fall asleep; the child keeps on nursing at intervals[Pg 224] until twice the proper quantity is taken; or she gives it the nipple or the bottle if it cries, without regard to whether it is the proper feeding time or not. The habit of overfeeding is very common in infants who are suffering from indigestion. They cry frequently, and are irritable most of the time; nothing seems to satisfy them but the nipple. Taking the warm milk into the stomach seems to allay the distress for the time being, so mothers get into the habit of quieting them in this way. The cry of the drinking man, whom we try to sober up, is: "Just one more drink and I'll quit." You give the drink and in a little while the demand is repeated. If the mother understood the seriousness of this practice of giving the child the nipple or bottle at irregular times, she would not do it.

Overfeeding an infant may lay the foundation for a lifelong ailment. The excess of food remains in the stomach or bowels undigested. If you remember that this mass of undigested matter is confined in a small space which is both warm and damp, it will be easily understood that putrefaction is the inevitable outcome. As a result of this putrefaction there are produced certain ptomaines and leucomaines. These poisons are carried through the body, causing "auto-intoxication" which upsets and irritates the child's nervous system and may cause very serious consequences, as it frequently produces sudden death from apoplexy and "heart failure" in the adult. These children are always restless, fretful, continually uncomfortable, sleepless and colicky. They lose weight, the stomach becomes distended and a gastritis or inflammation of the stomach results.

Frequently a mother with such a fretful baby, seeing her child getting thinner and thinner, will think that it is not getting enough to eat, and will proceed to add to the trouble by giving the child more to eat.

Mothers must therefore learn not to overfeed their infants; not to imagine that a failure to gain weight means the need of more food (if the quality of the food being given is wrong, will increasing the quantity of bad food do any good?); not to feed irregularly, no matter how insistent the child may be.[Pg 225]

Intervals of Feeding.—The physician will give instructions regarding the feeding of the newly born baby for the first few days. After the first few days and up to the beginning of the third month, it should be fed every two hours from 7 a. m. until 9 p. m., and twice during the night between 9 p. m. and 7 a. m., when the regular two-hours' interval again begins for the following day. The two night feedings should be about 1 and 4:30 a. m.

After the third month, and up to the sixth month, feed every three hours and once during the night. From the sixth month until weaned, every three and one-half or four hours, and not at all during the night.

While it has been pointed out that regularity of feeding is absolutely essential, the above schedule is not to be regarded as an absolute guide. It is a general guide,—approximately it will be found correct in a large majority of cases. Each baby is a rule unto itself. The quantity of the mother's milk will dictate the interval after the first month and for each month as the baby grows. If a mother with no milk to spare, is nursing a big, strong, husky baby, the three-hour interval during the day may have to be shortened to two and one-half hours. As a rule, however, these exceptions are better regulated by attention to the time the baby is given at each nursing to fill its stomach.

How Long Should a Baby Stay at the Breast?—Babies differ as to their method of feeding; some of them seem to like to nurse a moment or two and then look around; others seem to regard nursing as a serious business, and resent any effort to take the nipple away until they have finished. A baby should be taught to nurse methodically; it should not be allowed to play the nipple. Let it fill its stomach and put it down as quickly as possible. A mother will very soon know just how long it takes the baby to fill its little stomach, and when she finds this out she should time it by the clock. When the supply of milk is sufficient, and the child is strong, and nurses freely, eight to twelve minutes are sufficient. After it is taken away from the breast it must be left quiet till the next feeding.

Other babies, according to the ability they evince to[Pg 226] nurse, even when the milk runs freely, require a longer time,—from twelve to fifteen minutes. The rule, however, is never to allow them to nurse so long that when they are taken away the milk runs out of the mouth. If this occurs, cut down the length of time they are at the breast, and always time the length of feeding by the clock,—don't guess at it.

Children Who "Vomit" Between Feedings.—When a child habitually brings up food between feedings it is usually a symptom of gastric indigestion. In these cases it is advisable to add lime-water to each feeding, and to remove some of the fat in each feeding. If improvement does not follow remove more of the fat by removing some of the cream from the top of the bottle before shaking it.

Remove from the bottle four ounces of cream and shake before preparing the food from what is left. If the child improves after a few days remove only three ounces, then in a few days remove two ounces and later one ounce. After a time, sufficiently long to permit the stomach to become accustomed to the graded amounts of fat, the former diet of whole milk can be again resumed.

Never decrease the interval of feeding of a baby who is bringing up parts of its meal between feedings; it is frequently advisable to increase the interval. If a child is colicky and is bringing up lots of gas in addition to some food, one-half grain of benzoate of soda may be added to each ounce of food given and continued for a number of weeks if necessary. When the gas is located in the intestines and is not brought up, it must be made to pass downward. Attention to the bowels is of great importance in these cases and it may be necessary to peptonize the milk for some time. A reduction of the sugar and starch in the feeding frequently cures this condition. (See "Colic.")

There are children who continue to have symptoms of indigestion and who do not thrive despite various changes in the quantity and quality of the feedings. It may be necessary to obtain a wet nurse for them, as it is with "the delicate child." If a wet nurse cannot be obtained,[Pg 227] or if the age will permit, a substitute may be tried. Borden's Eagle brand of condensed milk, canned, is probably the best substitute under these circumstances. Condensed milk should never be used as a continuous food; as a substitute, however, for a few weeks it is often invaluable. With an infant of three or four months it should be used at the beginning in the proportion of one ounce of the milk to sixteen ounces of plain boiled water or barley water. The proper quantity, whatever the child is taking (four or six ounces according to the age) at the time, can be taken from the sixteen ounces and fed to the child. As the symptoms improve the milk should be diluted less and less, 1 to 14, 1 to 10, and so on until the proper strength is reached. After the child has been on the condensed milk for a month it should be changed back to cow's milk, using of course a diluted formula until the child becomes accustomed to the change. Condensed milk, if used as a permanent food, will fatten babies, but their vitality is very deficient, the muscles flabby, and the resistance to disease exceedingly poor. They are apt to develop rickets and sometimes scurvy.

Regularity of Feeding.—One of the very first, and one of the most important factors in contributing to the good health and the comfort of a baby is absolute regularity in feeding. A regular interval of feeding is particularly essential during the first month of a baby's life.

Despite the explicit way in which young mothers are instructed in this respect, it is one of the disappointing incidents of the practice of medicine to observe how many of these mothers fail to heed the advice. We have personally tried to find an explanation for this astonishing carelessness, and have come to the conclusion that it is not due to intentional forgetfulness, but rather to an inexplicable failure to appreciate that the physician means exactly what he says.

If, for example, specific instructions are given to feed, or nurse, the child every two hours (and by "specific instructions" it is meant, that the physician takes time to explain in detail the instructions he gives—that the[Pg 228] instructions are not incidental to the call, but part of the call;—that the advice is given not as a choice of what is desirable, but as an absolute rule to follow; and carefully explains why it is imperative to do as he says; and is satisfied the mother understands what he means) it would seem that there could be no possible reason why the directions should not be faithfully carried out. Yet such is not the case in many instances, and the excuses given by mothers for failure are so trivial and annoying that they show a failure to appreciate that they are dealing with a serious problem—a problem affecting human life. They fail to understand that fatal consequences may follow their negligence. They treat the baby problem exactly as they would a household incident, and as they do not consider it important whether the breakfast dishes are washed at 9 a. m. or at twelve noon, neither do they consider it important whether the baby is fed at 9 a. m. or an hour later. When mothers learn that the attention they must give their babies is essentially different from the attention they give ordinary household duties, the problem of raising children with success and comfort will be greatly simplified.

If the instructions are to feed the baby at certain intervals, do so at all hazards. To offer the foolish excuse that the baby was asleep when feeding time came, is no excuse at all; as a matter of fact the baby should be asleep at each feeding time, if it is healthy. Wake it and feed it, for, as will be shown later, it is the constant regularity that counts. It will be more difficult to institute regular feeding intervals during the first month, because a healthy baby is very difficult to wake up, even to be fed, during the first few weeks of life. It is absolutely essential, however, that it should be wakened: otherwise the tendency to overfill the stomach at the next feeding will lead to indigestion and colic.

Why is Regularity of Feeding Important?—Because a baby's stomach holds a very small quantity, and experience has taught us that a baby will thrive better on small quantities given frequently, rather than large quantities at longer intervals. The smaller the baby, the smaller the quantity to begin with. Some babies weigh from[Pg 229] five to seven pounds at birth, while others weigh from nine to twelve pounds. It would be unreasonable to expect a very small baby to be able to hold and digest as much as a very large baby. Considerable common sense and the exercise of some judgment is therefore necessary on the part of the uninstructed mother, as to just the right quantity to give. Fortunately, a little experience will enable the observant mother quickly to solve this important problem. Nature promptly furnishes the symptoms which will correctly guide her. Before considering the significance of these symptoms let us appreciate certain facts common to all babies, and we will more easily interpret the meaning of the special symptoms the baby will furnish.

First of all the baby never vomits. The ejection of food, therefore, is dependent upon a condition, not a disease. If milk runs out of its mouth immediately, or within a few moments, after a feeding, the explanation is that it was fed too much; it does not vomit, the stomach simply overflows. It is exactly like trying to put more milk into a cup after it is full,—it will not hold more, it overflows.

The significance of this symptom, therefore, is that the quantity of the feeding is wrong (it is not the baby's stomach that is at fault,—it is the mother's judgment). Reduce the quantity of each feeding and you will quickly cure it. If the milk does not overflow soon after a feeding, the baby will appear satisfied and will go to sleep, and will sleep until it is time for the next feeding. It may not do this, however. In half an hour, or a little longer, after the feeding, it wakes, it begins to fret and cry, and very soon it suddenly belches gas and ejects a mouthful of milk, after which it will rest quietly for a few moments, when it will begin fretting all over again. It may keep up this performance for an hour, or until the next feeding, and if so it is exhausted and unfit to carry on the digestive process. It is in these cases where most mothers make serious mistakes. This is the beginning of real trouble, and the family physician is the only one qualified to give advice under such circumstances. Remember the warning given regarding heeding the advice[Pg 230] of every busybody just at this time. Your baby's health is at stake; maybe its life depends upon what you choose to do.

What is the Significance of "Vomiting" After Feedings in Babies?—Let us examine the difference between the milk which overflowed immediately after the feeding and the milk which the baby ejects one-half hour or so later, and which is now being considered.

The first milk looks like ordinary milk (breast milk), or if the baby is being fed from the bottle, it looks just like the mixture in the bottle. It not only looks like what it took, but it smells just like it. Now examine the other; we find it looks like curdled milk, it is lumpy, and we immediately can tell that it is sour, because it smells sour and looks sour.

The explanation of the first overflow (immediately after the feeding) was the too great quantity; the explanation of the second overflow (one-half hour or so after the feeding), is the wrong quality of milk. The quantity was right because none overflowed right after the feeding, but the quality was wrong. Again, it is not the baby's stomach that is at fault,—it is the quality of the milk.

How do we know this? Because of what takes place in the baby's stomach during the one-half hour between the feeding and the time of the overflow of the sour milk. The quantity being right, why should the baby have any trouble if the quality is correct? It should not. Therefore by changing the quality (not the quantity as in the former case) we cure the trouble, thus proving the quality of the milk to be at fault.

What took place in the baby's stomach in the intervening half hour? The quality being wrong, the little stomach could not digest the mixture quick enough. Fermentation set in, gas was evolved, and as the stomach was full before the gas was manufactured (and as more and more gas is manufactured when food ferments), the stomach overflowed and out of the baby's mouth comes gas, and sour, fermenting, curdled milk. This process goes on until fermentation stops, or until the little stomach has just enough left to fill it and no more. But think what this is,—a sour mass of rotting, indigestible,[Pg 231] curdled milk,—and that is what this baby is expected to live and thrive on.

Some babies seem to have trouble from the very first day of life. Either they will not retain the food, or the food fails to agree with them. If the baby is put upon artificial food at once, these troubles are, of course, not unexpected (because the right artificial food may not be first chosen for the particular baby), but it is not always the artificially fed baby that gives us trouble, and it is sometimes difficult to find the cause for such trouble in a baby who has had nothing but its mother's milk since it was born.

The cause of stomach trouble in a baby a few days old, fed exclusively on mother's milk, is invariably to be found in the quality of the milk.

The quality of the mother's milk may be affected in a number of ways which will render it unfit for the baby. For example, if the mother for any reason becomes sick, and has a high fever shortly after confinement, it will affect her milk and render it unfit temporarily.

If the mother worries or becomes highly nervous during the first few days of her baby's life, she will so affect her milk as to render it unfit for baby. If a baby is fed for a number of days after its birth by its mother, and it should prove afterward that she has not enough milk to continue feeding it, and has finally to put it on artificial food, the baby will most likely have acquired slight stomach ailments that may be troublesome for some time, because in this case both the quality and the quantity were no doubt wrong. Constipation in the mother will also cause trouble. The child will develop colic and extreme irritability until the mother's condition is relieved.

Each of these conditions affecting the milk of the nursing mother usually demands a change of food for the baby, and the substitution of the proper artificial food will invariably immediately correct the trouble. In some cases, however, the quality of the mother's milk is not dependent upon a temporary temperamental condition, but is caused by errors in diet, or conduct, or both. The milk of a physically tired, worn-out mother, is not good, no matter whether the exhaustion is caused by actual[Pg 232] physical labor or by the exactions of a strenuous social programme. The milk of a mother who persists in eating irregularly, or who willfully caters to an appetite which craves the rich, highly seasoned articles of diet, or who attempts to satisfy a legitimate hunger by drinking large quantities of stale tea or coffee and eating bread, is unfit for her baby.

These cases are amenable to the proper treatment, which of course means, that the mother must change her conduct if at fault, and live strictly upon the diet prescribed elsewhere for nursing mothers.

If these troubles occur in babies who have been fed exclusively upon artificial food, an entire change of food is frequently necessary.

FRESH AIR FOR BABY

Baby's first journey out of doors depends upon so many contingencies that no specific age can be given when it would be perfectly safe to take it.

First, the weather and season of the year should be considered. The baby should not be taken out at all when it is wet, or foggy, or very humid; nor when it is extremely cold.

Second, the vigor or vitality of the individual child must be considered. Some children can safely be taken out if the weather is propitious when two weeks old, others cannot be taken out without risk until they are two months old, regardless of the weather conditions. If a child is robust at birth, and nurses well, and increases in weight from the beginning, he can be taken out when he is two weeks old while the sun shines during the middle of the day. If a child is small and puny when born, and begins to have nursing troubles from the beginning, does not increase in weight, is fretting, and crying, and sleeps spasmodically, it would be unsafe to take it out before the sixth week unless it is at a season of the year which would justify exposure to the sunshine.

The question of suitable clothing will be important, and will decide the advisability as to when the baby should go out. Every baby should be dressed in wool[Pg 233] weather is not too distinctly bad. Remember always to [Transcriber's note: words missing in text] from neck to ankles. Its head should be warmly clad. Dressed thus and well wrapped in blankets, a healthy child is ready for an out-door trip at any time, if the [Transcriber's note: words missing in text] have plenty of blankets below the child as well as above it, if it is in a baby carriage. In very cold weather the child should be buried in blankets, and a hot water bottle can be wrapped in near his feet. Great care must be taken that the water in the bottle is not too hot, and that it does not actually touch the skin. No matter how many or how few blankets are used, the face should be exposed directly to the fresh air. When the air is very gusty, or high, a light veil can be laid over the face, but never at any other time.

Air Baths for Babies.—Babies necessarily require plenty of exercise and plenty of fresh air, as has been pointed out. It is a splendid custom to allow the baby to lie naked after his bath for half an hour. If the room is comfortably warm, select a spot that is free from draughts, and lay the baby on a pillow or two and let him kick and coo. In the sun by the window, his head and especially the eyes shaded from the direct rays of the sun, is an excellent place in the summer time. The influence of the direct sun rays on the little naked body is conducive to good sturdy health, good nerves, and sound sleep.

[Pg 235]

CHAPTER XVIII

BABY'S GOOD AND BAD HABITS. FOOD FORMULAS

Baby's Bed—The Proper Way to Lay Baby in Bed—Baby Should Sleep by Itself—How Long Should a Baby Sleep—Why a Baby Cries—The Habitual Crier—The Habit of Feeding Baby Every Time it Cries—The Habit of Walking the Floor with Baby Every Time it Cries—Jouncing, or Hobbling Baby—Baby Needs Water to Drink—The Evil Habit of Kissing Baby—Establishing Toilet Habits—Baby's Comforter—What can be Done to Lessen the Evil Effects of the Comforter Habit—Beef Juice—Beef Juice by the Cold Process—Mutton Broth—Mutton Broth with Cornstarch or Arrowroot—Chicken, Veal, and Beef Broths— Scraped Beef or Meat Pulp—Junket or Curds and Whey— Whey—Barley Water—Barley Water Gruel or Barley Jelly— Rice, Wheat or Oat Water—Imperial Granum—Albumen Water—Dried Bread—Coddled Egg.

BABY'S BED

The Proper Way to Lay Baby in Its Bed.—The baby should be accustomed to sleep by itself from the day of its birth. Mothers have been known to smother their babies during sleep. The mother may pull the bed-clothing over the baby's head during the night and thus deprive it fresh air. A mother is much more apt to nurse her baby regularly and to do it more efficiently, if she is compelled to get up to do it. If she occupies the same bed with baby, she may fall asleep while nursing him; the baby consequently nurses too long, fills his stomach too full, and soon develops indigestion and colic in addition to acquiring a very bad habit.

For the first few weeks an ordinary basket arrangement is all that is necessary. As soon as the baby begins to move around it should have a regular baby crib, so that possible accidents may be avoided.

When the baby is placed in bed after a feeding, it should be laid upon its back, being tilted slightly toward its right side. By placing a soft, small pillow, under its[Pg 236] left side, the baby will rest more on its right side, which is the proper position. The reason of this is because the liver of a child grows quicker and larger than any other organ, and it is on the right side. By placing the child on this side, it prevents the heavy liver from sagging over on the little full stomach. If the child were laid on its left side, the liver would crowd the full stomach and embarrass the heart, and cause pain and restlessness. Frequently a change of position fully to the right side, when a child has been restless or crying, and especially if it has been lying on its back, will at once relieve it and allow it to go to sleep again. It is the knowledge of these little things that count in babyhood.

How Long Should a Baby Sleep?—A perfectly healthy baby should sleep, while very young, eighteen or twenty hours out of the twenty-four. As it grows older it will sleep less. It should have, and nothing should interfere with its having, two sound naps every day,—one in the forenoon after its bath, and the other in the afternoon. When four or five months old, it should also sleep from 7 p. m. until 10 p. m., then it should be fed and allowed to sleep until morning. It has been aptly said, that, "a child might easily overeat, but he practically never oversleeps." During the second year a child should sleep twelve hours at night, and about two hours during the day. The twelve-hour night rest should be continued until the child is six years of age. The practice of taking a nap at noon is a very good one, and it should be encouraged as long as possible. It can usually be kept up until the child begins school life. The strenuous activity of childhood, makes some such rest highly desirable, and the result will necessarily be a stronger body, a better disposition, and firmer nerves than otherwise. The practice of retiring early should be strictly enforced during childhood. Children of two years of age, should retire at 6:30 p. m., or at latest at 7 p. m., those from three to five years, may remain up an additional hour. At thirteen or fourteen the regular bedtime should be at 8:30 p. m. There is no justification for the late hours which growing children are allowed to keep, especially in large cities.[Pg 237]

Regular sleep is largely a matter of habit, and if the infant is started right, with suitable feedings, given at definite times, followed by the proper periods of sleep, but little trouble will be experienced with sleeplessness. When sleep is disturbed and broken, it means bad habits, unsuitable food, minor forms of indigestion, or positive illness of some kind. Sleep is absolutely essential in infancy and all through childhood for purposes of growth. It is wrong to permit a child to sleep too much during the day; it will become a habit, and it will not sleep well during the night as a consequence. In order to prevent or break this habit, the child should be kept in a well-lighted room and should be amused and entertained so as to keep it awake. The nap during the middle of the day is an exceedingly important factor in keeping the average child in good physical condition. It is a valuable adjunct in preventing, and in treating, nervousness in children. Children who are anemic should be encouraged to sleep long and freely in well-aired rooms.

Why a Baby Cries.—As has been stated, every healthy baby should cry for half an hour each day. Nature suggests, demands this as an essential exercise. Muscular movements involving a greater part of the whole body accompany the act of crying and furnish this necessary exercise. It is of great importance to an adequate and uniform development of the lungs; deep breathing is necessary to lusty crying, hence the lungs are expanded and the blood renewed and oxygenated. Crying is also of material aid in moving the baby's bowels. Babies in perfect health will, however, cry under any of the following circumstances, and doubtless under circumstances of lesser importance and frequency when frightened or uncomfortable from hunger or position, soiled napkins, inflamed buttocks, earache, pain, from heat or cold, unsuitable clothing, and during difficult bowel movement, when displeased or angry. Children slightly but painfully ill may cry incessantly for an hour or two. Thus, with intestinal colic, when the cry is loud and continuous until the child is relieved or until he falls asleep from exhaustion.

The healthy, well trained child seldom causes trouble;[Pg 238] it is the rule for it to be happy and good natured in its own way.

The Habitual Crier.—If a child becomes a habitual crier, it is because it is uncomfortable and unhappy. There are restless, often vigorous, crying, whining infants, and the trouble, as a rule, is in the intestinal tract. Badly managed, "spoiled babies" cry from inattention, and when left alone. If they are taken up and talked to, the crying ceases, thus proving that it was not pain or discomfort that was causing the crying. In the case of the habitual crier we try to find out the cause of the bowel trouble and cure it; the spoiled infant we discipline rigidly, or leave it alone if its parents prefer that kind of baby.

The Habit of Feeding Baby Every Time It Cries.—The habit of regular feeding will, if persisted in and successfully established, render advice on this subject unnecessary. So also will the explanation of the evil of overfeeding have its effect on mothers. Apart from these reasons, however, the habit of feeding baby every time it cries is a pernicious one, and no doubt the mother, who will be striving to faithfully follow instructions, will have to overcome the advice of meddling friends who will regard it as a cruelty to allow the baby to cry. Do not give in to these busy-bodies; insist on attending to your own affairs, but be absolutely sure baby is not crying for a just cause. A child can only cry; that is its only language, but it cries for many things other than the nipple or the bottle. Examine it carefully,—a wet diaper a pin, an uncomfortable position, a drink of water, any of these may be the cause.

It is just as essential that a child should cry as that it should sleep. Every healthy child should cry for twenty or thirty minutes every twenty-four hours. Nature calls for this as an exercise in order to develop the lungs; therefore, if there is no just cause for the crying you must regard it as a necessary evil, even if you look upon it as a domestic affliction.

The Habit of Walking the Floor With Baby Every Time It Cries.—This is another habit that is indulged in to the sorrow and ridicule of the race. If you are a[Pg 239] victim of this habit, you have yourself to blame. It is a matter of education, or habit, pure and simple, and, like all bad habits, it is difficult to break away from. In the preceding paragraph, you have been told that when baby wants something, or is uncomfortable, it employs the language nature gave it,—it cries. No child ever cried to be walked up and down the floor in the dead of the night. Begin at the beginning, when it first cries, find out why it is crying. Offer it a little water if it is not feeding time. Examine its diaper and if soiled change it. It may be overdressed and consequently hot, perspiring, and uncomfortable; change its position. Find out if any pin is open and hurting it; loosen the binder so it can breathe easily. If it is a colicky child follow the instructions given in the treatment of colic. Be patient the first few nights, and be thorough, because you may discover why it cries and each discovery will help you next time. If you discover something wrong, some reasonable excuse for the crying, does it not prove the folly of walking the floor? If it wants a drink of water, or if its diaper is wet, how is walking the floor going to cure it, or how can you expect the baby to stop crying when you so unjustly construe its reasonable and its only way of asking a favor? If walking the floor stops its crying, it stops it by exhausting the child, not by relieving it of its little ailment.

Jouncing or Hobbling Baby.—This is another habit that should be frowned upon. So many persons are addicted to this form of baby torture, that it is astonishing more immediate harm does not result from it. Be particularly careful not to indulge in it, or permit anyone else to do it immediately after feeding. If you form the habit of putting baby down at once after each feeding, as you have been instructed to do, the opportunity to jounce it will not exist. A little reasoning will clearly convince you that to subject a baby to violent exercise when its stomach is full would interrupt digestion and so shake the full stomach hat it would distend it and cause indigestion. You would not think of exercising yourself after a meal; why exercise a baby?

Baby Needs Water to Drink.—Boil a quantity of[Pg 240] water each morning, put in a clean bottle, and keep in a cool place. Give the baby some, three or four times daily between feedings. One teaspoonful is enough to begin with, and as it grows older it will take more. It may not always take the water but it will take what it wants, and it needs some every day; it is therefore your duty, inasmuch as baby cannot ask for it, to offer it regularly each day as part of your daily routine.

KISSING

A child should never be kissed on the mouth by anyone, not even its own parents.

Kissing should not be allowed among children. If any kissing is done it should be on the brow, never on the mouth, hands, or fingers.

Many diseases are carried by this pernicious habit, and you cannot afford to have baby's health jeopardized by this promiscuous and unnecessary liberty.

ESTABLISHING TOILET HABITS

When baby reaches the age of three months, a regular systemized effort should be made to educate it to "habits of cleanliness." Nothing can be done in this direction previous to this age, as a child at that period of its life is scarcely conscious of the natural functions of its body. Each time a baby, after the third month, is making an effort to move its bowels, the nurse or mother should go to it as it lies in its crib, and talk to it by making a certain sound or say a certain word—whichever word or words you want to educate your child to say, when it wants to move its bowels. By constant attention and effort in this direction, a child with quick perception and initiative will soon associate the sound and the function, and it will begin to make the sound when the function is about to be performed. As soon as it begins to make this sound, if prior to the act of moving the bowels, the child should be immediately taken up and held on a chamber, into which some hot water has been put, and encouraged to[Pg 241] relieve itself, the nurse or mother still repeating the sound, or word, or words.

Having successfully accomplished this programme a number of times, the child should be encouraged and petted every time it gives a satisfactory warning, and discouraged and reproved every time it wets or soils its napkin. A little later, say about six months, the child should be held on the chamber at a certain time each morning and evening, thus encouraging it to move its bowels regularly twice daily. The careful carrying out of a scheme such as the above will establish regular, cleanly habits, and will to a very large extent guard against constipation in the future.

Baby's Comforter.—The discovery and introduction of the comforter or rubber teat was an unfortunate episode in someone's life. By the careless, conscienceless nurse, or thoughtless mother, it is regarded as a real comfort and blessing. Any temporary comfort, however, which the nurse or mother may enjoy as a result of its use, is at the expense of the health of the child. Its use is a serious reflection upon the good intention and intelligence of the mother who permits her child to use one. It is a bad habit from every viewpoint possible. In order that mothers, open to conviction and capable of reasoning, may appreciate the character of the harm done by the use of the comforter, we will briefly record these conditions:

1st. The constant sucking pulls upon the delicate structures of the mouth and throat, and so impairs the health tone of these structures that they become flaccid and feebly nourished. This to a certain degree causes adenoids, enlarged tonsils, loose palate and weak throat, with the constant tendency to winter colds and coughs, and to catarrh.

2nd. It causes an excessive flow of saliva. Saliva should only be stimulated previous to stomach digestion. By causing an excessive flow of saliva into an empty stomach, the digestive powers are interfered with, and seriously weakened. Stomach trouble, and consequently intestinal disease, may therefore be caused by the seemingly innocent comforter.[Pg 242]

3rd. A constantly used comforter always causes disease of the mouth. Mucous erosions, canker sores, little ulcers, etc., are produced in this way.

4th. The use of the comforter makes it impossible to put the child to sleep, or even to leave it alone, without first placing it in its mouth.

5th. To stifle a baby's cry, by pushing the comforter into its mouth, is as bad as giving it chloroform to mask a serious and dangerous pain. If may have a just reason for crying, as is explained elsewhere, and if that reason is not searched for and found, it may mean serious trouble later.

6th. Actual deformities of the mouth are produced by constant use of the comforter. The continuous sucking affects the gums, pushes them out of shape and position, and the teeth as a consequence come at wrong angles, thus causing unsightly deformities, which last throughout the life of the child.

7th. The worst fault of the comforter is to be found in its uncleanliness. We are quite satisfied that the use of the comforter will be legislated against one of these days. If preventive medicine means anything, it must certainly reckon with the comforter in the very near future. Have you ever watched your baby suck on its comforter? If you have, you must have noted the tireless energy with which it works its tiny jaws and tongue. Suddenly the comforter slips from the little mouth and baby begins to cry, attracting the attention of the mother, or nurse, or little sister, who promptly, recognizing the trouble, pounces on the offending comforter, which has fallen to the floor, and with a perfunctory wipe replaces it in baby's mouth. It is done just as we have written it, many thousand times, and yet the problem of infant mortality is represented as a vexatious mystery. The newspapers solicit charitable aid, and write eloquent appeals regarding the necessity of sending a few babies to the seashore in the summer time or to supply a few with ice during the hot spells. A hundred other energetic enthusiasts send forth their laudable effort to raise the standard of child hygiene, yet the manufacturers of the comforter, and the ignorant mother and nurse who use it,[Pg 243] do more harm in one day than all the honest effort of these combined forces can neutralize in a year.

The rubber comforter is one of the most fertile causes of infection and illness in babies because of the peculiar adaptability to collecting germs which it possesses.

When the comforter is finally discarded the habit of sucking is so firmly established that the child will suck its thumb for many years after. This results in further disease and deformity to the growing mouth and throat, and also to the thumb.

After a child has used a pacifier or comforter for some time it invariably becomes a mouth breather. A mouth-breathing child is very apt to catch cold and as a consequence of the habit may become catarrhal or tubercular.

What Can be Done to Lessen the Evil Effects of the "Comforter" Habit?—It is a most difficult habit to cure when once established. The very least that can be done is to keep the comforter scrupulously clean, washing it several times daily. To have not one, but two or three, kept in a saturated solution of boracic acid, ready to put into the baby's mouth should one be required to replace another that has fallen out. We should furnish a large shield to prevent it being swallowed. We can try the method of weaning the baby from the comforter by tying a ribbon to it and to the child's bodice. The system is gradually to shorten the ribbon until it becomes too short for the baby to suck in comfort. It will then gradually grow away from the habit.

FOOD FORMULAS

Beef Juice.—Take one pound of round steak and broil it slightly. Press the juice out with a lemon squeezer, or, with a meat-press. Season with salt and serve hot or cold as desired. If it is heated after it has once been cold, it should not be overheated as this will coagulate the albumen which will appear as flakes floating on the surface of the juice.

Beef Juice by the Cold Process.—Take one pound of finely chopped round steak, six ounces of cold water, a pinch of salt; place in a covered jar and stand on ice, or in a cool place, six hours. This mixture should be shaken from time to time. Strain and squeeze all the juice out by placing the meat in a coarse cloth and twisting it very hard. Season and feed as above.[Pg 244]

Beef juice made in this way is more nutritious than that made from the steak when broiled; it is not, however, quite so palatable.

Beef juice made in either of the above ways is much more nutritious than the beef extracts sold ready to use.

Mutton Broth.—Take one pound of finely chopped lean mutton, including some of the bone, one pint of cold water and a pinch of salt, cook for three hours over a slow fire down to half a pint, adding water to make up this quantity if necessary; strain through muslin. When it is cold remove the fat and add more salt if required. It may be fed warm or cold in the form of a jelly.

Mutton Broth With Cornstarch or Arrowroot.—Add to the above sufficient cornstarch or arrowroot to thicken, cook for ten minutes and then add three ounces of milk, or one ounce of thick cream, to a half pint of broth. This makes a nutritious and extremely palatable broth.

Chicken, Veal, and Beef Broths.—These may be made and used in the same way as mutton broth.

Scraped Beef or Meat Pulp.—Take a rare piece of round or sirloin steak, cut the outer part away, scrape or shred with a blunt knife. Cutting the meat into small pieces is not satisfactory. One teaspoonful to one tablespoonful may be given well salted, to a child a year and a half old. It is best to begin with a small dose and work up to the larger to accustom the digestive apparatus to its use.

Junket, or Curds and Whey.—Take one pint of warm fresh cow's milk, a pinch of salt, a teaspoonful of granulated sugar, to which add two teaspoonfuls of Fairchild's essence of pepsin and allow the mixture to stand until firmly coagulated—this may take about twenty minutes—place in the ice box until thoroughly cold. Nutmeg may be added for older children and adults.

Whey.—The coagulated milk prepared as above is broken up with a fork and the whey is strained off through cheesecloth. If a stimulant is desired, brandy, in the proportion of one teaspoonful to six tablespoonfuls of the whey may be added.

Barley Water.—One level tablespoonful of Robinson's barley is rubbed up with a little cold water, to this is added one pint of boiled water containing a pinch of salt. The mixture should be stirred while the water is being added. Cook for thirty minutes in a double boiler and strain. Enough boiling water should be added to the mixture to make up the full pint if any has boiled away.

Barley Gruel or Barley Jelly.—Repeat the above process, but instead of using one tablespoonful of the barley powder, use from two to four according to the consistency of the gruel or jelly desired.

Barley water may be made from the grains. A formula for this process will be found in the chapter on artificial feeding.

Rice, Wheat, or Oat Water.—These are made from the rice,[Pg 245] wheat, or oat flour in the same way as barley water described above. They may be made from the grains also, using the same proportions as in the making of barley water.

Imperial Granum.—This is prepared in the same way as the barley flour above described.

Albumen Water.—Take half a pint of cold water, the white of one fresh egg, a pinch of salt, and a teaspoonful of brandy, shake and feed from a spoon or from a bottle. This is frequently used in cases of vomiting, or in irritable stomachs. It is often retained when all other food is rejected.

Dried Bread.—Cut either stale or fresh bread into thin slices and place in the open oven. When it is dried and crisp but not browned it may be given to children in preference to crackers.

Coddled Egg.—A fresh egg with the shell intact is placed in boiling water which is immediately removed from the fire. The egg is allowed to remain in the water for eight minutes when it is ready for use. The white only should be used if the digestion is poor.

ARTIFICIAL FEEDING

[Pg 249]

CHAPTER XIX

ARTIFICIAL FEEDING

Elementary Principles of Milk Modification—The Secret of the Efficiency of Mother's Milk—Two Important Factors in Successful Artificial Feeding—Every Child is a Problem in Itself—Proprietary Foods of Little Value as Infant Foods—Their Value is in the Milk Added to Them—The Credit Belongs to the Cow—Difference Between Human and Cow's Milk—What "Top-milk Feeding" Means—Utensils Necessary for Home Modification of Milk—Artificial Feeding from Birth to the Twelfth Month—How to Measure Top-milk—Easy Bottle-feeding Method—Condensed Milk Feeding—Objections to Condensed Milk Feeding.

Elementary Principles of Milk Modification.—Mothers who have to raise their children on artificial food should understand the elementary principles of milk modification. They should know, for example, that the one object of milk modification is to render it as nearly an exact substitute for mother's milk, according to the age of the child, as is possible. If we could do this with scientific exactness, artificial feeding would be a simple process. We cannot, however; nor has there ever been devised a method by which we may hope successfully to duplicate mother's milk. It is a comparatively simple matter for the efficient chemist to analyze the breast milk of any nursing mother; and it is quite possible to duplicate the milk according to the analysis, with chemical exactness, but the two fluids will not be the same. There is present in the mother's milk something which synthetic chemistry cannot discover. This something is nature's secret,—it is akin to the life-giving principle which is contained in the germinal fluid, and in the hen's egg. We cannot therefore hope to build up an artificial food that contains this mysterious life-giving principle which is the secret of the efficiency of maternal milk,—we can only hope to approximate it.[Pg 250] It is possible that we might be successful so far as its nursing efficiency is concerned, if all children were alike, if all children were of a uniform standard of health. As a matter of fact, no two babies are exactly alike. And while the mother of each child undoubtedly secretes a milk suitable to the degree of healthfulness of her own child, the same milk might not be equally suitable to another child. The milk, therefore, that is manufactured to agree with an average mother's milk is dependent for its success upon the vitality of the child to which it is fed. If that child is not a well child, according to an accepted standard, the milk will not agree with it, even though it is the best possible substitute for an average breast milk.

We have consequently two factors to consider in successful or efficient artificial feeding:

1. Our inability to duplicate exactly mother's milk. 2. The lack of a uniform health standard in children.

It is the lack of a uniform health standard in children that gives to artificial feeding all its difficulties. It renders the successful artificial feeding of children a personal or individual problem. Some children,—those who approximate a standard of health for their age; in other words, "well" children,—thrive on a milk modification that experience has taught us is suitable for well children of their age. Others, and they are in the majority, have to be fed on a modification which actual test proves to agree with their digestive capabilities. Every artificially fed child therefore must be studied from its own individual standpoint. A certain modification of milk may not agree with a child fed every two and one-half hours, which will be found to agree if fed in the same quantity, to the same child, every three hours. The slightest change, a change which would seem to be so insignificant in itself as not to justify serious consideration, may mean the difference between normal healthfulness and constant ill health. A food that is too strong for a child's digestive ability, and which causes vomiting, colic, and diarrhea, may be rendered exactly right by the slightest modification one of its constituents. To effect such a change quickly[Pg 251] and successfully, one must be trained to interpret the symptoms correctly and to know how to make the change in the modification of the milk. Mothers cannot be expected to possess this degree of skill: they should therefore refrain from experimenting, because an experiment on a baby is not only dangerous, but ethically it is criminal. Call the family physician; put the burden on his shoulder.

It is this element of uncertainty in our ability to effect a standard modification of milk that has afforded manufacturers the rich opportunity of putting on the market various baby foods for which much is claimed. These foods are really substitutes for the inefficiency of the average mother. There is no real justification for their use. If all mothers were clean, faithful, and efficient, there is no reason why each one could not be taught to modify cow's milk to suit her child, just as satisfactorily, or more so, than a manufacturer who never saw her child. The manufacturers, however, do the work, and the naturally ignorant or lazy and inefficient mother, is willing to pay for the extra cost of labor, to save herself the trouble on the one hand, and to subject her child to a series of experiments in order to discover the manufactured food that is particularly adapted to her particular baby on the other hand. We believe that most mothers have never considered the question from this standpoint; that most mothers adopt this method of artificial feeding at the direct suggestion of their family physician, and are not, therefore, responsible. These foods do not contain the nutritional elements necessary to healthy growth; or as they exist in normal breast milk; or as they can be approximated in ordinary milk modification at home. Proprietary foods are of decidedly poor value in infant nutrition, and should not be used. They have a value, however, in certain diseased conditions, but within a very small range. As a food for a healthy growing infant, they should not be used, and when the average physician appreciates this fact, and so instructs the mothers of the country, it will be to the distinct advantage of the race in every respect. Proprietary foods to which fresh[Pg 252] cow's milk is added, are not foods at all,—they depend upon the milk so far as any nutritional value is concerned; and it would be far safer to modify at home a good milk than to buy a proprietary food, the analysis of which cannot be depended upon. The credit for the fat, healthy babies we see advertised does not belong to the manufacturers, but to the cow whose milk you add to the manufacturer's sugar.

The proprietary beef foods are also valueless as infant foods. In certain illnesses, when we want a mild stimulant, a teaspoonful or two in hot water may have a certain value, but that is all. The beef juice of home manufacture is much more valuable.

Difference Between Human and Cow's Milk.—The composition of cow's milk is as follows:

Fat (represented by cream)   4%

Sugar   4%

Proteids (represented by curd) 4%

The composition of an average human breast milk is as follows:

Fat   4%

Sugar   7%

Proteids 1-1/2%

It will be observed from a comparison of the above tables that cow's milk is much richer in proteids (the substances which form with water the curd of sour milk) than is human milk. If one remembers that cow's milk is manufactured by nature primarily for the feeding of calves, not for babies, and that the stomach of a calf is intended to exist exclusively on vegetable products, and that nature is preparing it for this purpose, and feeds it a food when young that will enable it to grow so as to be adapted for that purpose, one can understand that the problem of the modification of cow's milk to suit the stomach of a baby is not by any means a simple matter. Since the proteids are so much in excess in cow's milk, we must dilute cow's milk with twice its bulk or more of water to render it fit food for a new born baby. If we dilute cow's milk to this extent to get the proteid percentage right, we immediately disarrange[Pg 253] the percentage of the cream or fat. We overcome this difficulty by taking the cream from the top of the bottle and diluting it because it is richer in fat and does not need so much dilution. This is the explanation of the so-called "top-milk feeding." The percentage of sugar represents another problem. The percentage of sugar in cow's milk compared with the sugar in human milk is deficient, so we add milk-sugar to the cow's milk to make up the deficient percentage.

There is yet another feature which we must rectify; cow's milk is acid, while human milk is alkaline. To overcome this difference we add lime-water. We must also take into consideration that cow's milk is ordinarily full of germs, while human milk is free from them; to overcome this danger we resort to heating the milk to a degree which experience has taught us will kill all germs. Cooked milk is not as wholesome as uncooked milk, and it has a tendency to cause constipation. We have to a certain extent overcome the need for cooking all milk for babies, as will be noted later, but in summer time, unless the milk is known to be pure and free from germs, it is advisable to sterilize it.

UTENSILS NECESSARY FOR HOME MODIFICATION OF MILK

One dozen round, eight-ounce nursing bottles. One dozen black rubber nipples. One eight-ounce measuring glass or graduate. One brush for cleaning bottles. One two-quart glass preserve jar for mixing the various ingredients. One one-ounce Chapin dipper, for removing the top-milk. One glass funnel.

A detailed description of the proper kinds of bottles and nipples will be found elsewhere. The measuring glass or graduate should be wide-mouthed. It is not safe to spoon the top-milk off, nor is it safe to pour it out. Absorbent cotton should be provided to close the nursing bottles when filled and left standing in the ice box.[Pg 254]

ARTIFICIAL FEEDING FROM BIRTH TO THE TWELFTH MONTH

The following formulas for the different ages may be found useful for well babies:

From the third to the tenth day:

Milk (top 16 oz.)   3 ounces.

Lime-water   1/2 ounce.

Milk-sugar   1 ounce.

Boiled water to make 16 ounces.

Ten feedings in twenty-four hours; 1-1/2 to 2 ounces at each feeding.

From the tenth to the twenty-first day:

Milk (top 16 oz.) 6 ounces.

Lime-water   1-1/2 ounces.

Milk-sugar   1-1/2 ounces.

Water to make   24 ounces.

Nine to ten feedings in twenty-four hours; 1-1/2 to 2 ounces at each feeding.

From third to the sixth week:

Milk (top 16 oz.) 10 ounces.

Lime-water   2-1/2 ounces.

Milk-sugar   2 ounces.

Water to make   32 ounces.

Eight to nine feedings in twenty-four hours; 2 or 3 ounces at each feeding.

From sixth week to the third month:

Milk (top 16 oz.) 12 ounces.

Milk-sugar   2 ounces.

Lime-water   3 ounces.

Water to make   32 ounces.

Seven to eight feedings in twenty-four hours; 2-1/2 to 4 ounces at each feeding.

From third to fifth month:

After this age two bottles of milk are required, 16 ounces being taken from the top of each bottle and mixed.

Milk (top 16 oz.) 18 ounces.

Milk-sugar   2 ounces.

Lime-water   4 ounces.

Water to make   40 ounces.

Six feedings in twenty-four hours; 4 to 5 ounces at each feeding.

From the fifth to the seventh month:

Milk (top 16 oz.) 21 ounces.

Milk-sugar   2 ounces.

[Pg 255]

Lime-water   5 ounces.

Water to make   42 ounces.

Six feedings in twenty-four hours; 5 to 7 ounces at each feeding.

From the seventh to the ninth month:

Milk (top 16 oz.) 27 ounces.

Milk-sugar   2-1/2 ounces.

Lime-water   6 ounces.

Water to make   48 ounces.

Five to seven feedings in twenty-four hours; 6 to 8 ounces at each feeding.

From the ninth to the twelfth month:

Milk (top 16 oz.) 30 ounces.
Milk sugar — 1½ ounces.
Lime water 6 ounces.
Water to make 60 ounces.

Five to six feedings in twenty-four hours; 7 to 9 ounces at each feeding.

It will be observed that 16 ounces of top-milk is used to make the various formulas from. This means that the mother will dip off, with a Chapin dipper, 16 ounces from the top of a bottle of milk which has stood for four or five hours to allow the cream to rise; she will then mix this and take from the mixture the number of ounces called for in the formula she is using according to the age of the child. The ordinary milk that is delivered in New York City may be assumed to have stood the four or five hours necessary. This may not be so, however, in the country, as it is frequently delivered there as soon as it is milked. In such cases the mother will permit it to stand in the ice box until the cream has risen.

When the mother is about to make the mixture called for in feeding from the third to the fifth month she will observe that 18 ounces of milk is called for. Now since she only uses 16 ounces of the top-milk from one bottle this will not be enough. She must therefore use 16 ounces from two bottles of milk; this she will mix together and from this mixture she will take the 18 ounces wanted. Whatever milk is left over may be used for ordinary table purposes.[Pg 256]

EASY BOTTLE-FEEDING METHOD

The following formulas and instructions for bottle-feeding are taken from the Rules for the Care of Infants and Young Children which are used by Dr. Kerley at the out-patient department of the Babies' Hospital and give the simplest and easiest means of bottle-feeding:

Bottle-Feeding.—The bottle should be thoroughly cleansed with borax and hot water (one teaspoonful of borax to a pint of water) and boil before using. The nipple should be turned inside out, scrubbed with a brush, using hot borax water. The brush should be used for no other purpose. The bottle and nipple should rest in plain boiled water until wanted. Never use grocery milk. Use only bottled milk which is delivered every morning. From May 1st to October 1st the milk should be boiled five minutes immediately after receiving. Children of the same age vary greatly as to the strength and amount of food required. A mixture, when prepared, should be put in a covered glass fruit-jar and kept on the ice. For the average baby the following mixture will be found useful:

"For a child under six weeks of age: Nine ounces of milk, twenty-seven ounces of barley-water, four teaspoonfuls of granulated sugar. Feed from two to three ounces at two and one-quarter hour intervals, nine feedings in twenty-four hours.

"Sixth to the twelfth week: Twelve ounces milk, twenty-four ounces barley-water, five teaspoonfuls sugar. Feed from three to four ounces at each feeding.

"Third to the sixth month: Eighteen ounces of milk, thirty ounces of barley-water, six teaspoonfuls of sugar. Feed four to six ounces at three-hour intervals, seven feedings in twenty-four hours.

"Sixth to the ninth month: Twenty-four ounces milk, twenty-four ounces barley-water, six teaspoonfuls granulated sugar. Feed six to eight ounces at three-hour intervals, six feedings in twenty-four hours.

"Ninth to twelfth month: Thirty-eight ounces milk, twelve ounces barley-water, six teaspoonfuls of granulated sugar. Feed seven to nine ounces at three and one-half hour intervals, five feedings in twenty-four hours."

Barley-Water.—The barley-water used in the above formulas may be made in the following way: To two teaspoonfuls of pearl barley, add one quart of water, and boil continuously for six hours, keeping the quantity up to a quart by the addition of water; strain through coarse muslin. The barley will be better if it is soaked[Pg 257] for a number of hours, or over night, before cooking. The water in which it is soaked is not used.

An equally good barley-water may be made in an easier way by using Robinson's prepared barley. This may be procured in the drug stores. It is only necessary to take one even tablespoonful of this barley to twelve ounces of water and cook for twenty minutes.

Condensed Milk.—When the mother cannot afford to buy bottled milk from the wagon, when she has no ice-chest and cannot afford to buy ice, she should not attempt cow's-milk feeding, but may use canned condensed milk as a substitute during the hot months only. The can, when opened, should be kept in the coolest place in the apartment, carefully wrapped in clean white paper or in a clean towel. The feeding hours are the same as for fresh cow's milk:

"Under three months of age: Condensed milk one-half to one teaspoonful; barley-water, two to four ounces.

"Third to sixth month: Condensed milk, one to two teaspoonfuls; barley-water, four to six ounces.

"Sixth to ninth month: Condensed milk, two to three teaspoonfuls; barley-water, six to eight ounces.

"Ninth to twelfth month: Condensed milk, three teaspoonfuls; barley-water, eight to nine ounces."

Objections to Condensed Milk Feeding.—Condensed milk is not to be recommended as a permanent food where good cow's milk can be obtained. In most cases it should be used as the sole food for a few weeks only. It may be used when the digestion is impaired for some reason. If the symptoms are intestinal it will be more apt to agree than if they are caused by stomach ailments. The symptoms of intestinal disturbances are,—colic, flatulence (gas), curds or specks in the stools, constipation or diarrhea. It will not be found suitable if the child is simply vomiting.

The objections to condensed milk are: It is very rich in sugar and very deficient in proteids and fat. Children fed on condensed milk often gain very rapidly in weight but have little strength or resistance. They do not fight disease well for this reason; they are apt to develop rickets and scurvy.

[Pg 259]

CHAPTER XX

ARTIFICIAL FEEDING—CONTINUED

How to Prepare Milk Mixtures—Sterilizing the Food for the Day's Feeding—How to Test the Temperature of the Food for Baby—When to Increase the Quality or Quantity of Food—Food Allowable During the First Year in Addition to Milk—Beef Juice—White of Egg—Orange Juice—Peptonized Milk—The Hot or Immediate Process—The Cold Process—Partially Peptonized Milk—Completely Peptonized Milk—Uses of Peptonized Milk—Objections to Peptonized Milk—What a Mother Should Know About Baby's Feeding Bottle and Nipple—Should a Mother Put Her Baby on Artificial Food if Her Supply of Milk, During the First Two Weeks is not Quite Enough to Satisfy it—Certain Conditions Justify the Adoption of Artificial Feeding from the Beginning—Mothers' Mistakes in the Preparation of Artificial Food—Feeding During the Second Year—Sample Meals for a Child Three Years of Age—The Diet of Older Children—Meats, Vegetables, Cereals, Bread, Desserts—Fruits.

HOW TO PREPARE MILK MIXTURES

The mother should always remember, that the secret of success in raising a baby efficiently on artificial food is to be cleanly and to be exact. The bottles and the nipples must be scrupulously clean; the hands of the mother must be clean; the water used must be boiled and each ingredient must be measured exactly.

First dissolve the sugar in the boiled water, which must be the exact quantity; then remove the top-milk and measure the exact amount wanted in the graduate, pour into the jar, add the water and sugar mixture, and finally the lime water.

It is always desirable to make the entire quantity for the day at one time. After the total quantity has been mixed in the jar, fill each bottle with the amount for each feeding, put in a cotton stopper, and place the bottles in the ice box.

In measuring the sugar, it should be remembered that[Pg 260] two scant dipperfuls equal one ounce by weight of the sugar.

When each individual bottle is to be filled, do it with the aid of the glass funnel which has been previously sterilized.

Sterilizing the Food For the Day's Feeding.—The simplest method is to place the two-quart jar containing the milk mixture for the next twenty-four hours' feeding upon a saucer in the bottom of an open pan, and then to pour enough tepid water into the pan (outside of the jar) until it will come up as high as the milk level. The water in the pan is then brought slowly to the boiling point. The pan is then moved to the back of the stove and left for half an hour. The jar is then removed and rapidly cooled by allowing cool water to flow over the outside; the individual bottles filled and put in the ice box.

It is always wise to taste the milk before making up the day's feeding to be sure it is not sour. The milk from a herd of good cows is always better than the milk from one cow no matter how good that one cow may be.

When about to feed the baby, the bottle is taken out of the ice box and heated to the desired temperature in a water bath. The temperature of the milk can be tested by allowing a few drops to fall on the wrist; it should feel warm, not hot; it should not be tasted by putting the bottle to the mouth of the nurse, or mother, as it may become infected by doing so. A flannel cover, or bag, should be made to fit the bottle and it should be put on while the baby is nursing so that the milk may retain its heat. The baby must not be disturbed while nursing, nor should he be jounced or carried around after nursing. These habits cause vomiting and indigestion. He should be put in his crib.

When to Increase the Quality or Quantity of Food.—Children of the same age may have different digestive abilities. A strong, robust child may be permitted to take a richer quality of milk than a weak, puny infant of the same age. If the quality or quantity of each feeding is too weak or small for the baby he will be dissatisfied[Pg 261] and he will cry after the feeding. In such cases, if the bowel discharges are natural and yellow without curds or white specks, and if he is not gaining sufficiently in weight, the next stronger formula may be tried. If it is decided to put him on the stronger mixture, it is wise to cut the quantity down for a day or two in order to test out his digestive ability. If the stools remain good after three days, the quantity may be slowly increased until the amount in the recipe is allowed. It is a much more serious risk to overfeed the baby than to underfeed him. If too large a quantity is given, he may vomit it at once, or he may develop colic with intestinal indigestion. Such babies lose weight, become fretful and irritable, even though the appetite may remain good. If too strong a quality is given he may vomit sour, buttery-smelling milk, or have colic, and pass curds in the stool. If this happens it may be necessary to go back to a weak formula and work up from that standard. This is always a tedious and anxious experience and may lay the foundation for digestive disturbances for a long time. Don't be too anxious to increase the quality, or quantity, of your baby's food. It is much better to go slow and have a well baby, than to try to force matters and get into all kinds of trouble. No science calls for more elementary common sense, than the science of infant therapy.

Digestive disturbances incident to this period are fully explained in the chapter on Diseases of Children.

FOOD ALLOWABLE DURING THE FIRST YEAR, IN ADDITION TO MILK

About the twelfth month the baby should receive plain milk mixtures instead of the top-milk heretofore used in making up the food. At first the milk may be plain milk from an ordinary bottle shaken up. Of this he may take five ounces, to which may be added three ounces of barley water. The barley water may be gradually withdrawn, an ounce at a time, replacing this amount with milk, until the child is taking eight ounces of milk and two ounces of barley water. Later plain mixed milk will be suitable for a child about the fourteenth month.

Barley water may be added to the milk at any time[Pg 262] after the third month in place of the plain boiled water in the preceding formulas. It is advisable to do this if there is any trouble with digestion, or if there are curds in the stools. Some children take more kindly to barley water than plain water at a very early age.

Beef Juice.—The juice squeezed from broiled steak may be given a child at about the eighth or ninth month, or, in cases of anemia, earlier than this. It is given before the milk feeding, diluted with an equal amount of water. At first a teaspoonful of the extracted juice should be given with the same quantity of water; increase every four days until at the end of two or three weeks two tablespoonfuls are given.

White of Egg.—Place an egg in boiling water and allow the water to cool with an egg in it. In ten minutes the white of the egg will be coagulated and ready for use. It may be used in place of the beef juice if the latter does not agree and may be begun at the sixth month and given once daily. One-half of the white of the egg should be tried, then at the end of a week, if it agrees with the child, the whole white of one egg may be given.

Orange Juice.—This juice has a good effect on the bowels and may be given even to very young children who are disposed to be constipated. It is also of benefit in counteracting the effect of boiled milk. The juice should be extracted from fresh oranges and strained. One teaspoonful may be given at first one hour before a feeding. The amount may be increased until four teaspoonfuls, or one tablespoonful, are given daily.

Peptonized Milk.—The object of peptonization of milk is partly or wholly to digest the casein, or curd, of the milk before feeding.

Fairchild's Peptonizing Powder is used for this purpose. The powder is put up in tubes, and instructions are furnished in each box as to its use.

There are two methods of using the powders:

The Hot or Immediate Process.—Fifteen minutes before feeding add from one-eighth to one-quarter of the contents of a tube to the milk mixture in the nursing bottle ready for use. The bottle is then put in water at a temperature of from 110° to 120° F., and allowed to[Pg 263] remain in the water for fifteen minutes. The amount of the powder used and the temperature of the water depend upon the amount of milk in the nursing bottle.

The Cold Process.—Four ounces of cold water are put into a clean quart bottle and the powder from one of the tubes. Shake the mixture thoroughly until the powder is dissolved. Add a pint of cold fresh milk, shake the bottle again and place directly on ice. When any of this milk is used the bottle should be again shaken and put immediately back on ice.

If necessary this process may be modified so that partially or completely peptonized milk may be made.

Partially Peptonized Milk.—Put four ounces of water and a whole tube of powder into a clean pan and stir well; add a pint of cold milk and heat to the boiling point, stirring the mixture all the time. There should be enough heat to bring the milk to the boiling point in ten minutes. Allow the mixture to cool somewhat and strain into a clean jar, cork tightly and keep in a cool place. Shake the jar before and after using any of the contents.

If partially peptonized milk is properly prepared it should not become bitter.

Completely Peptonized Milk.—Put four ounces of cold water and the powder contained in one of the tubes into a clean quart bottle and shake thoroughly. Add a pint of cold fresh milk and shake again; then place the bottle in a pan of warm water about 115° F., or not too hot to place the hand in comfortably. Keep the bottle in the water bath for thirty minutes; then place the bottle directly on ice.

Uses of Peptonized Milk.—Partially peptonized milk is useful in young infants who have difficulty in digesting the curd of milk. Completely peptonized milk is frequently used during attacks of indigestion. It is used also to tide a delicate infant over a period when for some reason the digestive apparatus refuses to digest and assimilate even dilute mixtures. It is of value also in acute or chronic illness when the child has to be fed through a tube. When it is necessary to feed per rectum peptonized foods are often selected in preference to others.[Pg 264]

Objections to Peptonized Milk.—Complete peptonization of milk renders the milk bitter. For this reason many children will not take it. Very young children whose sense of taste is not developed may be induced to take it after a few days. It is not wise to continue its use long because the function of the stomach will become accustomed to the use of predigested food and refuse to work when called upon. If it is used for a number of weeks it is wise to stop it gradually in order to permit the stomach to resume its function in a normal way.

What a Mother Should Know About Baby's Feeding Bottle and Nipple.—In the first place, always buy round bottles,—round everywhere, inside and out,—there should be no corners anywhere. The reason for this is, that bottles that are round everywhere, are easily cleaned, and can be thoroughly cleaned, and having no corners they do not lend themselves to collecting dirt and bacteria. When these bottles are first bought they should be boiled. After each feeding they should be thoroughly washed with soap or washing powder. A long-handled bottle brush should be used to help clean the bottle. After the bottle has been thoroughly rinsed a number of times with hot water, it should be set aside filled with warm water into which one teaspoonful of bicarbonate of soda has been put. Before filling them with the freshly prepared food each morning the bottles should be boiled. Every mother with a bottle-fed baby should buy a dozen bottles, all of the same kind and size to begin with. This is a great advantage for a number of important reasons, two or three of which I will mention:

1st. Having enough bottles means that each bottle will be used once only during the twenty-four hours; there is less chance therefore of a bottle being cleaned carelessly.

2nd. Having a fresh bottle for each feeding permits all of the food for twenty-four hours being made at one time. This ensures uniformity of quality of each feeding.

3rd. By cleaning all the bottles at one time (previous to filling) it is more apt to be done thoroughly; and by making all the food for a day at one time it is more[Pg 265] apt to be correct than if each feeding was made separately.

The baby's nipple should be made of plain black rubber. It should not be too thick because it is necessary to turn it inside out in order to clean it thoroughly. The hole in the nipple should not be too large—if the child can empty the bottle in less time than fifteen minutes the hole is too large. If the milk drops out but does not run it is about right. Don't buy nipples too long or too large. A long nipple tends to gag the child and cause vomiting. A large nipple prevents the child from sucking properly and usually allows the food to be taken too quickly and with air, which causes colic and indigestion. It is well to have always half a dozen nipples of the right kind on hand. When new, nipples should be boiled before using. After each feeding the nipple should be washed in borax and water on both sides, then it should be put in a dish containing fresh, cold, borax water and left there until again required. A large portion of the success of raising healthy, bottle-fed babies is in being everlastingly clean in the details of caring for the bottles and nipples which are in daily use.

Should a Mother Put Her Baby on Artificial Food if Her Supply of Milk, During the First Two Weeks, is Not Quite Enough to Satisfy It?—This is a question that cannot be answered by a simple yes or no. A great deal depends upon circumstances, and these circumstances must be weighed and counterweighed before an answer is given. It is a serious matter, in our judgment it is a criminal proceeding for a physician to advise the use of an artificial food without exhausting every aid and means to preserve and increase the mother's milk. This is a subject in need of earnest missionaries in all walks of life, and it should be the duty of every woman's club and gathering to voice the conviction of the highest womanhood by advocating the use of mother's milk with every child born. A woman who can and will not nurse her own child is scarcely deserving of the name of mother.

It does not seem quite human to deprive a baby of the milk which rightfully belongs to it; yet in certain walks of life this is not an uncommon procedure. On the other[Pg 266] hand the percentage of women able to nurse their children is decreasing. This is especially true as applied to cities, though it is also true, in a less degree, in the rural districts. One eminent authority states that less than twenty-five per cent. of the well-to-do mothers, who have earnestly and intelligently attempted to nurse their babies, succeed in doing so for a period longer than three months. This authority also says: "An intellectual city mother who is able to nurse her child successfully for the entire first year is almost a phenomenon." Women nowadays have so many diversified interests, that the primal duty of maternal nursing is not at all a fashionable function. If, however, the mother is willing, and has conscientiously tried to nurse her baby, and after seven or eight days it is found that she has not enough milk to satisfy it, and if the quality seems to be good, some expedient should be immediately adopted to tide the condition over until the mother resumes her customary household routine. The safest expedient under these circumstances is to alternate the feedings; one feeding from both breasts of the mother, and the next an artificial food. Some arrangement of this kind is the just and the safest way, because a very large percentage of mothers suffer from inactivity while lying in bed after a confinement. This inactivity expresses itself in a failure of some of the organs to perform their duty properly. This may affect the quantity, and sometimes the quality, of the milk, but it is, as a rule, quickly rectified as soon as the mother is up and active.

If, however, the milk is still found to be inadequate after she is up and has resumed her usual habits, and if her health is good, and she is eating well, it is distinctly best to put the child exclusively on an artificial diet.

CERTAIN CONDITIONS JUSTIFY THE ADOPTION OF ARTIFICIAL FEEDING FROM THE BEGINNING

1st. Woman suffering with any wasting disease such a cancer or tuberculosis. (One of these days, and very soon we hope, it will be legally impossible for a tubercular or cancerous patient to become a mother.)[Pg 267]

2nd. When a mother is the victim of any of the serious childbed complications such as convulsions, kidney disease, extensive loss of blood or blood poisoning, or runs a high temperature because of some disease occurring at the same time as the confinement, as, for example, appendicitis, scarlet fever, typhoid fever, etc.

3rd. Epilepsy, chorea, insanity, are also conditions which render artificial feeding necessary.

It is much wiser immediately to put the child on artificial feeding if there is a justifiable reason for it than to experiment, because any experiment at this time is almost certain not to be in favor of the child. Artificial feeding is a comparatively easy and successful problem, provided it is begun with healthy digestive organs. If you keep the child at the breast of a mother whose milk is inadequate in quantity or quality, or both, for two or three days, and then begin artificial feeding, the child's stomach is already unable to perform its duty, and you have to treat it with the greatest degree of care and attention, and probably begin with a weak food, until you regain the lost ground.

Mothers' Mistakes in the Preparation of Artificial Food.— Another interesting condition which is quite common, is the tendency on the part of the mother to fail to follow instructions correctly,—even though written or printed,—regarding the preparation of the baby's food. When the baby is not thriving and gaining steadily in weight, or is fretty and cries a good deal, and does not rest and sleep peacefully, something, of course, is wrong. If, after a careful physical examination of the child, nothing is found to justify these symptoms, a physician invariably finds, if he questions the mother closely, that she has mistaken the instructions and is preparing the food wrongly.

Infinite care in every little detail is the price of success in raising babies as well as in every other field of human endeavor. Revise carefully your method of preparing baby's food if there is any trouble such as is described above. Despite your absolute assurance that you are making no mistake, do not be surprised to find that you are not following directions to the letter, and because of[Pg 268] this unintentional mistake, your negligence is responsible for your baby's condition. Go over the instructions with your husband, and let him follow your method of preparation, as you repeat it. He may detect the mistake if any exists,—two heads are always better than one. So important is this matter that the following two actual cases will demonstrate how easy it is to make a mistake, despite the absolute confidence of the mother, in each case, that she was following the printed directions correctly:

I was called to see a baby whose mother informed me that it was having a great deal of trouble. It was apparently not thriving; its bowels were bad; it constantly cried, and seemed to be suffering from colic and indigestion. The mother stated that it lay with its legs constantly drawn up and passed enormous quantities of gas. The baby certainly looked sick. It had been a small baby at birth; and at three months it weighed only six pounds. After a careful examination, I could find nothing in the physical condition of the child itself, which satisfactorily explained the condition, and had made up my mind that the food upon which it was being exclusively fed, and upon which it had been fed since birth, was not agreeing with it. Before recommending a change of food, I asked the mother to state in detail just how she prepared it.

The directions printed on the can in which the food was bought called for so many ounces of a certain quality of "top milk." She thought this meant simply so many ounces off the top of a bottle of milk, which, of course, meant that she was feeding her baby exclusively a very rich cream and absolutely no milk. The result was that the baby—small and weak to begin with—could not digest this rich mixture, so it gradually lost vitality, as the mother kept increasing the strength of the food, according to the age, as directed by the instructions, until it was completely knocked out. I pointed out her mistake and suggested a change in her methods; she was instructed to use the formula for a child of two months, instead of the one for three months, as she was doing. The child immediately began to pick up and in the course of six weeks was entirely cured, and had gained considerably[Pg 269] in weight. This mother was a careful, clean, painstaking, attentive nurse, and it was a long time before she forgave herself for the mistake. The mistake here was a little matter, but the results were big and convincing.

The second case was that of a child of about the same age, but in this instance it had been a robust, healthy child when born, and of normal weight and size. The mother nursed it for about one month, when her milk failed, and it was put upon a well-known, patent barley preparation. The food seemed to agree with it for a time, but, as the mother explained, the child soon seemed to be dissatisfied at each feeding,—it gave her the impression that it was not getting enough to eat, so she increased the quantity. Despite this increase of food, it was apparent that the baby was getting weaker, and more and more irritable, and sleepless, until there was no rest night or day for the mother or baby. About this time the child began to "swell up" as if dropsical; it lost its healthy color and looked as if made of wax. It was very evident that the child was being starved, yet this scarcely seemed probable when the actual quantity of food consumed was considered. The directions on the can of this food, called for a certain amount of the barley powder to be mixed with boiled water; and in an additional paragraph it was directed to mix this with a certain amount of milk. When I requested the mother to state how she prepared the food, I was astonished to learn that she had evidently never read the second paragraph of the directions. She was feeding her baby on barley powder and boiled water,—an excellent starvation diet. When her attention was called to the grave carelessness she had been guilty of, she was the most contrite mother I ever knew. As soon as the milk was added to the food the baby immediately began to thrive was very soon a robust, healthy infant.

Of course these were errors of bad judgment and gross negligence of which few mothers would be guilty, but these types of mistakes come to the attention of physicians frequently, and emphasize the need of constant vigilance in every detail in the management of babies if we wish to achieve success.[Pg 270]

FEEDING DURING THE SECOND YEAR

At the beginning of the second year the child should be fed at the following hours, 6 and 10 a. m., 2, 6, and 10 p. m.

Early in the second year the child should be taught to drink from a cup.

A proper diet for a child of twelve months, of average development, would be as follows:

6 a. m. Milk and barley water, or milk and oat gruel, in the proportion of seven ounces of milk to three ounces of the diluent.

9 a. m. The juice of an orange (strained).

10 a. m. The same as at 6 a. m.

2 p. m. Chicken broth with rice or stale bread crumbs, six ounces; or a light boiled egg mixed with stale bread crumbs; or

beef juice, three ounces. Milk and gruel same as at 6 a. m., but four ounces only.

6 p. m. Two tablespoonfuls of cereal jelly in eight ounces of milk; a piece of stale bread and butter. (The jelly is made by cooking the cereal for three hours the day before it is wanted; it should then be strained through a colander; oatmeal, barley, or wheat may be used.)

10 p. m. Same as at 6 a. m.

About the fifteenth month the cereals may be given much thicker and fed with a spoon. The child can at this time take a number of various fruit juices. Orange juice is the best. Carefully strained juice of ripe peaches, strawberries, raspberries, may be given in reasonable amounts, one or two tablespoonfuls, once daily. Custard, cornstarch, plain rice pudding, junket, wheatena, cornmeal, hominy, oatmeal, zwieback, bran biscuit, each with butter, may be added in reasonable quantities between the eighteenth and twenty-fourth months. When cereals are given they should be thoroughly cooked, usually for three hours, and strained. When apple sauce is given to a child about the second year it should contain very little sugar and baked apples should be fed without cream. Water must be given to the child between meals especially during the summer. It should be boiled and cooled kept in a cool place. The following schedule for a child about the third year constitutes a good average diet for a healthy child:

TABLE OF STANDARDS

(As Adopted and Copyrighted by the American Medical Society)

PHYSICAL DEVELOPMENT

[Transcriber's Note: The ages were difficult to read and may not all be correct.]

Age in Months	Weight	Height	Circumference of head	Circumference of chest	Circumference of abdomen	La Di of

	lbs.	in.	in.	in.	in.	in
6	17	27	17-1/2	17-1/2	17-1/2	5
9	19	28	18	18	18	5
12	20	29	18-1/2	18-1/2	18-1/2	5
16	23	30	18-1/2	18-1/2	18-1/2	5-
21	24	31	18-1/2	19-1/2	19-1/4	6
24	25	32	19	20	19-1/2	6
28	27	33-1/2	19	20	19-1/2	6
32	29	35	19-1/2	20-1/2	19-1/2	6-
36	32	36-1/2	20	21	20	6-

MENTAL DEVELOPMENT

Attention, facial expression, irritability and disposition should be considered.

Six Months

Child sits unsupported for a few minutes.... Balances head.... Eye follows a bright object.... Looks in direction of an unexpected sound.... Child seizes an object and holds it....

Twelve Months

Stands and walks with support.... Makes a few sounds, such as mam-mam, da-da, co-oo.... Plays with toys.... Attempts to use paper and pencil.... Shows interest in pictures.... Clings to mother....

Eighteen Months

Child walks and runs alone.... Says a few words, such as Mama, Papa, Baby.... Points to common objects in pictures.... Imitates a few simple movements, such as placing hands on head or clapping hands....

Two Years

Runs.... Repeats two or three words.... Knows features.... Obeys simple commands, such as "Throw me the ball".... Imitates movements....

Two and One-Half Years

Talks in short sentences.... Knows names of members of the family.... Roughly copies a circle.... Recognizes self in mirror.... Imitates more complex movements....

Three Years

Talks distinctly.... Repeats sentences of six simple words.... Repeats up to two numerals—meaning repeats first one numeral and then two numerals.... Enumerates objects in a complex picture and attempts to describe it....

Four Years

Knows its sex.... Names familiar objects, such as key, knife, etc..... Repeats three numerals.... Compares two sticks (can select the longer).... Distinguishes the longer of two lines....

Five Years

Compares weights and lengths.... Copies a square.... Counts four pennies.... Describes a picture....

[Pg 271]

Breakfast:—(7 to 8 o'clock) Oatmeal, hominy or cracked wheat (cooked three hours), served with milk, a little salt but very little sugar. A soft egg, boiled, poached, or coddled. Stale bread and butter. One glass of warm milk. At 10 o'clock, the juice of one orange.

Dinner:—(12 o'clock) Strained soup, four ounces. Chop, roast beef, steak, chicken, small quantity of any one. Baked potato and cooked rice, or spaghetti. A selection of green vegetables may be made from asparagus tips, string beans, peas, spinach, cauliflower, carrots; they should be cooked until very soft, and mashed or put through a sieve. For dessert, plain rice pudding or bread pudding, stewed prunes, baked or stewed apple, junket, custard or cornstarch. A glass of milk or water.

Supper:—(6 o'clock) Cereal; farina, arrowroot, cream of wheat, wheatena (each cooked two hours), with salt but no sugar. Give two or three tablespoonfuls. Drink of milk with stale bread and butter. Twice a week, a little plain ice cream, or junket, custard or cornstarch.

Three meals a day at this time are better than more frequent feedings. The child has a better appetite and much better digestion. It may be found necessary to give delicate children a luncheon at 3 o'clock. A glass of milk and a Graham wafer, or a cup of broth and a zwieback, will answer the purpose. Children recovering from serious illness will need more frequent nourishment. Up to the sixth year the diet may conform to the above schedule, increasing the individual quantities as circumstances may warrant.

THE DIET OF OLDER CHILDREN (FROM SIX TO TEN YEARS)

After the sixth year the diet will conform to the adult diet, with certain exceptions. The important exceptions are as follows: All meats are to be excluded except roast beef, steak, lamb chops, roast lamb, mutton chop; all meats should be cooked rare and either scraped or finely[Pg 272] divided. They should be broiled or roasted, never fried, and never given oftener than once daily, and then only in small quantity. Pies, rich puddings, pastries of all kinds, gravies, sauces, all highly seasoned dishes; wine, beer, coffee, tea, should never be given to children. Ham, bacon, sausage, pork, liver, kidney, game, and all dried and salted meats, codfish, mackerel and halibut, are particularly bad.

The following articles are permissible: Broiled chicken, shad, bass. The "platter gravy" from a roast is very nourishing if given in small amounts. Milk should continue to form an important part of the dietary up to the tenth year. It should be clean and fresh but not too rich. Sometimes it is found advisable to dilute the milk with water that has been boiled and cooled. Some children will take it if a pinch of salt or bicarbonate of soda is put into it, and they will digest it easier and better. They should never be allowed to take more than one quart daily and frequently less will do more good. Cream is not good for children of this age. Eggs are valuable; they should never be given fried or in the form of omelets, they are best given boiled, poached or coddled and only slightly cooked. It is never necessary to give more than one egg at a meal. There are children with whom eggs do not agree; these children are disposed to "biliousness."

Vegetables.—Certain vegetables are objectionable at this age: Raw celery, radishes, raw onions, cucumbers, tomatoes, lettuce, corn, lima beans, cabbage, egg plant. The following are good: White potatoes (never fried), spinach, peas, asparagus tips, string beans, celery, young beets, carrots, squash, turnips, boiled onions and cauliflower. It is important to remember that all vegetables should be thoroughly cooked; they cannot be cooked too much. After boiling for some time the water should be drained off and fresh water used to complete cooking. Vegetables should be fed in small quantities. From the third to the tenth year they form an important and essential part of the diet of all children. After the tenth year they can be eaten as served to adults, and other vegetables may then be[Pg 273] added. As a rule salads of all kinds should be omitted until after the twelfth year.

Cereals.—Children should not be allowed to eat too much cereal at one meal,—never more than one small saucerful. Cereals should be properly cooked. It is not safe to adhere strictly to the directions on the package of any cereal. As a rule they require much longer cooking. They are best cooked in a double boiler. They may be served with milk, salt, and not more than one teaspoonful of sugar.

Bread.—Fresh bread is never allowable. Graham wafers, oatmeal crackers, Huntley and Palmer breakfast biscuits, bran muffins, rye bread, corn bread, stale rolls, are all suitable to growing children.

Hot bread, fresh rolls, buckwheat or griddle cakes, all sweet cakes, are objectionable.

Desserts.—The only permissible desserts for this age are junket, custards, plain rice, or sago; or bread pudding. The only safe rule to follow so far as "sweet things" are concerned, is not to give them at all. This applies to candy, ice cream, pies, pastries, jam, syrups, preserved fruits, nuts and dried fruits. The parent who indulges a child to "a taste," is guilty of a bad habit, and it can only lead to trouble.

Fruits.—These should always be fresh and selected with care. Fruit is the most important article of diet to a child of this age. Up to five years it is safest to use only cooked fruits and fresh fruit juices: of these the juice from sweet oranges, grape fruit, peaches, strawberries, and raspberries may be given. Stewed or baked apples, apple sauce, figs, prunes, peaches, apricots, pears are excellent because of their effect on the bowels. When the bowels are loose, and especially in hot weather, great care must be taken when fruit of any kind is used. The pulp of any fruit should never be used; cherries, bananas, pineapples, and berries are not to be given to children. Milk should never be allowed at the same meal when sour fruit is served.

WHAT MOTHERS SHOULD KNOW

[Pg 277]

CHAPTER XXI

"Life has taught me that it is the women of a country in whose hands its destiny reposes. No cause that is not great enough to command their devotion and pure enough to deserve their sympathy can ever wholly triumph."

Joseph H. Choate.

THE EDUCATION OF THE MOTHER

What Mothers Should Know About the Care of Children During Illness—A Sick Child Should be in Bed—The Diet of the Sick Child—A Child is the Most Helpless Living Thing—The Delicate Child—How to Feed the Delicate Child—How to Bathe the Delicate Child—Airing the Delicate Child—Habits of the Delicate Child—Indiscriminate Feeding—Poor Appetite—Loss of Appetite—Treatment of Loss of Appetite—Overeating in Infancy—What Correct Eating Means—Bran as a Food—Breakfast for a Child at School—Lunch for a Child at School—Bran Muffins for School Children—Bran Muffins in

Constipation—Hysterical Children—What a Mother Should Know About Cathartics and How to Give a Dose of Castor Oil—Castor Oil—Calomel—Citrate of Magnesium—When to Use Castor Oil—When to Use Calomel—Vaccination—Time for Vaccination—Methods of Vaccination.—Symptoms of Successful Vaccination.

WHAT MOTHERS SHOULD KNOW ABOUT THE CARE OF CHILDREN DURING ILLNESS

Every child has a certain amount of vitality and resistance. When illness comes it should be our duty to maintain the vitality and resistance to the highest degree. We should, therefore, irrespective of the nature of the illness, surround the child with all the conditions that will minister to the preservation of whatever strength and vitality the child has. Experience has taught us that there are certain requirements that should be carried out in the general management of sick children.

A Sick Child Should be in Bed.—In the first place a sick child should be in bed. There is no exception to[Pg 278] this rule. It is impossible to do justice to a child if you allow him to dissipate his strength and exhaust himself moving from place to place while he is sick. A mother should not forget that it is she who must exercise wisdom and decide what is best for her child. The judgment of a sick person is not to be relied upon, and it would be wrong to submit to the whims and fancies of an ailing child, if these are known to be medically disadvantageous to its best interests.

Quiet surroundings are essential in all acute illnesses. The nurse should be congenial to the child. If the patient demands the presence of the mother she should remain, but she should not try to entertain him or interfere with the nurse.

The clothing of the patient should be the ordinary night-dress which is worn in health. In no disease is any special kind, or quantity of clothing required.

The temperature of the room should be 68° F. Thermometers are cheap and an exact knowledge of the degree of heat in a sickroom is an essential requisite. Nothing drains the vitality during sickness quicker than varying degrees of heat and cold. It uses up nerve force and energy and renders the patient irritable and difficult to manage.

The strictest attention should be paid to the ventilation of the sickroom. We are learning more and more that fresh air is essential to the speedy cure of all diseases and to the general well-being of the patient. A direct, continuous communication between the sickroom and out-of-doors is imperative. It is a splendid measure to use two rooms for the patient and to change him twice daily, and to air thoroughly the unused room.

The sickroom itself should be large and in a quiet part of the house. In summer time the windows may be wide open, in winter months the degree of ventilation can be regulated by the thermometer.

Many mothers fail to appreciate that drinking water is an important requisite in all ailments of childhood, should be given freely, but it should be known to be absolutely pure. The same rule applies to sponging the patient. It must be done every day; sometimes it is[Pg 279] necessary to do it more often, but if so it will be so directed by the attending physician.

The Diet of the Sick Child.—Prescribing the diet of the sick child is an important undertaking. It should be remembered that during sickness the digestive capacity is reduced; consequently the food must be lessened in quantity and in strength. If the patient is an infant at breast the best way to accomplish our purpose is to give before each feeding two ounces of boiled water, cooled to the temperature of the body. This dilutes the mother's milk and renders it more easy of digestion. If bottle-fed, it is accomplished by replacing one-half of the milk with water. In certain diseases milk is totally withdrawn, but these cases will be noted when discussing the treatment of the various diseases. With older children, we give milk diluted with water, or gruels, soups, or cereals, as conditions warrant.

Needless interference with the patient must not be indulged in. Sleep and quiet are essential features of nature's reparative process. It is seldom necessary to disturb a sick child for the giving of food or medicine oftener than every second or third hour. Medicine may always be given with food. Meddlesome interference, talkative attendants, or excessive noise may exhaust a child and may prolong and render dangerous or fatal a condition that would otherwise go on to recovery.

One satisfactory movement of the bowel daily is essential to the comfort and progress of a sick person. If this does not take place naturally, it should be obtained by an enema.

At the beginning of any illness in childhood it is a safe procedure to give a dose of a suitable cathartic as soon as it is discovered that the child is sick.

A Child is the Most Helpless Living Thing.—Nature endows the young of every species—except those of the human family—with certain instincts, which, when developed, govern and control their lives absolutely. The technical definition of an instinct is an exceedingly complicated word picture. It is only essential to an intelligent understanding of our subject that the reader should have a definite idea of the difference between an act that[Pg 280] is the result of a process of reasoning and an act that is the result of an instinct. If a man finds his way out of his burning home he will stay out as long as there is any danger. The crudest kind of reasoning will teach this lesson. A horse, on the other hand—and incidentally it may be noted that a horse is regarded as an intelligent animal—if led out of a burning stable and let loose, will immediately reënter and be burned to death. The horse is the victim of instinct; he obeys the unconquerable instinct to return to his stall—he cannot reason as the man can that a home that is burning is not a proper place to seek safety in. When an ostrich fears danger he buries his head in the sand, under the impression that if his head is out of sight he is safe from danger. This is his instinctive plan of procedure in the presence of danger, and it is the plan of every ostrich, everywhere, always. A little reasoning would show them how foolish the idea is—but they cannot reason. That is the province of man alone. If the first member of a flock of sheep jumps over a fence to get into the next field, every member of the flock will follow, each one jumping the fence, though there may be an open gate between the two fields a few yards away. Instinct dictates the plan to the sheep as they have received instructions from their ancestors always to "follow the lead." This is their hereditary legacy and they cannot disobey it.

Animals are born with instincts which need only circumstances to bring them out. Now a baby is not born with instincts of this character,—it has not even the instinct to help itself; it cannot find the breasts that were made for it; it is more helpless than the baby cat or dog or worm. Therefore a baby in whose brain the potential faculty of reason is slumbering must of necessity begin its career wholly dependent upon the supervision and love of its mother, until such time as it may be capable of reasoning for itself. Motherhood is therefore the supreme privilege of womanhood. It cannot be superseded, hence the fundamental factor in any system of race culture, or in any system of infant mortality, must tend to raise the quality and the intelligence of motherhood[Pg 281] as a basic necessity. Motherhood at the present time, though the most important and sacred profession in the world, is almost exclusively carried on by unskilled labor. The maternal instinct is deeply rooted and universal; its absence must be regarded as an abnormality, or as a product of misdirected education. The requisites for the mothers of the future should be absolute physical health and love of children.

If nature endowed a baby with instincts there would be no need for reason or education. Education cannot teach a cat how to nurse or wash a kitten any better than it does,—its instinct is good enough. The mother of a human baby, however, is not born with the instinct which enables her to care for her baby equally as well as the cat cares for her kitten. She must be educated or taught to care for it. She can then care for it better than the cat cares for the kitten, and she can be taught to bake, to sew, to read; to play on the piano, which a cat cannot be taught. So while a baby may be the most helpless living thing at one stage of its career it has in it—in the faculty of reasoning—the ability to become the Lord of all the Earth and of all the animals therein. To limit the environment of a child by imposing instincts upon it, would be to limit its inherent freedom. To be obliged to obey a prescribed instinctive law would rob mankind of his creative or reasoning faculty, and that would be to lower him to the level of the brute creation. Reason is of no use if our acts are already determined for us. There are therefore good reasons why the human baby should be, at the moment of its birth, the most helpless living thing; and as a consequence it is imperative, if the eugenic ideal is worthy of attainment, that every baby should have the benefit of trained and efficient care and education.

THE DELICATE CHILD

There is a certain standard by which we measure the physical and mental development of children. This standard we regard as the evidence of normal development. Some children exceed these requirements; they[Pg 282] are bigger and stronger at a given age than the average child at the same age. There are other children who cannot be called sick, but who are physically and mentally inferior to the average standard, whom we designate as "delicate." These children are not as big, or as strong, or as heavy, as other children of the same age. They are born with a reduced vitality, or through mismanagement in early infancy they have acquired a subnormal standard of development. Children born of parents who are not of standard vitality are predisposed to be delicate. If the parents are of average development, and the delicacy of the child is acquired by mismanagement, the proper dietetic and hygienic management will, as a rule, promptly result in a satisfactory restoration to normal health.

Treatment.—When a mother awakes to the knowledge that her child is delicate; when she understands that her child's vitality is not what it should be, and when she resolves to "do something" in the interest of her child, she is on the right road, and we hope to encourage her in the good intention. We would however tell her that her effort must be thorough, and that she must be patient and persevering. If she does not falter in well doing she will succeed beyond her expectation, and the satisfaction she will experience in noting the evidences of returning health and strength in the appearance and conduct of her child, should be ample recompense for the effort made and the time bestowed.

She must begin with a definite knowledge of just what she intends doing; she must know, however, what must be done and she must begin at the beginning and build from a sure foundation. It is therefore absolutely essential to ascertain if there is any actual disease underlying the reduced vitality which is responsible for the delicacy of the child; this necessitates a thorough examination by a competent physician. If you are assured there is no disease present, no tuberculosis, no syphilis, no malaria, and that debilitating conditions, such as adenoids, sexual abnormalities, the results of self-abuse, skin disease, do not exist, then certain fixed rules can be laid down, and definite principles followed in the daily management.[Pg 283]

Weight, as a Standard of Development.—It has been stated elsewhere in this book that one of the safest guides to follow, as to whether a child is thriving, is its weight. This can be relied upon as a general rule. A child should therefore be weighed regularly every week. If it is not gaining an average of four ounces weekly it is not thriving up to standard. When the average is below four ounces there is something wrong with the quality or quantity of the food.

How to Feed the Delicate Child.—If the child is breast-fed and the weight standard, as evidenced by the weekly averages, is persistently below normal, we must find a substitute for the mother's milk. If the child is bottle-fed and it is demonstrated that it is impossible to maintain normal development on cow's milk, a wet-nurse should be obtained. After the child is weaned, or put upon a more liberal diet, milk should continue to be the chief article of diet. From the first to the third year a child should take one quart of milk daily in addition to the other food. There are some children, however, who seemingly cannot take milk without getting indigestion; they should be put on skimmed milk, to which may be added a small quantity of sugar to make up for the loss of fat. Mothers must be certain that too much milk is not given, or the desire for other necessary food will diminish.

After the first year it is a very good plan to give one teaspoonful of scraped beef daily. If this is well borne, two may be given and later three. It can be given immediately before the regular feeding of cereal and milk. From the twelfth to the sixteenth month eggs may be given: at first one-half, and later a whole egg mixed with bread crumbs. Various vegetables should also be given cooked in the form of a purée. If at any time the child should refuse the food, or act as if it had no appetite, leave the milk out of the diet; this may then restore the appetite and it will take the other food freely; the milk can be resumed later.

As the child grows older, the distaste for milk may grow, or he may be one of those children with whom milk really does not agree; in either event, do not hesitate[Pg 284] to leave it out of the child's dietary. These children should be encouraged to eat plenty of good butter on their bread and crackers. Butter will not only agree with them, but it will supply any fat deficiency in the general diet. The diet may now consist of milk (unless it disagrees), cereals cooked three hours, raw or rare meat, poultry, eggs, vegetables, purées, cooked and raw fruit, bread, crackers.

How to Bathe the Delicate Child.—Regular daily baths are particularly of benefit to the delicate child, despite the prevailing fear that they may catch cold. The salt bath is advised and the time to take it is just before retiring. The room should be warm and the temperature of the water should be 90° F.: it should not last longer than five minutes, and the water should be cooled down to 70° F., before the child is removed from the bath. While the cold water is running in, the surface of the body should be briskly rubbed with the mother's hands and after removal the child should be dried with a fairly coarse bath towel to ensure a good reaction. Very delicate children need not have the temperature of the water reduced; others may stand water of 80° F., but no lower. In the poorly nourished it is frequently advantageous to rub the body, after drying, with olive oil or goose oil. This aids nutrition and because of the massage it aids circulation. In some older children a daily cold spinal douche seems to act particularly well. If the child does not promptly react from the effect of the cold water it is best to discontinue it.

Airing the Delicate Child.—Delicate children should, above all things, be assured of the maximum amount of fresh air and sunlight. Many mothers entertain the idea that these children are disposed to take cold easily, if in the open air,—which is not the case. All children need an abundance of fresh air and the delicate need it particularly. The season of the year and the character of the weather will, of course, dictate just how much open-air exercise they may take.

If the weather is very cold and the air damp, or if there is a very cold high wind, it is best to remain indoors; otherwise the child should remain out for four[Pg 285] or five hours. Indoor airing is obtained by dressing the child to go out-doors, putting him in his carriage, and leaving him before an open window in a room of good size with all the doors closed so as not to create a draught.

Habits of the Delicate Child.—The amount of sleep necessary for a delicate child is the same as for a normal child of the same age. The room should always be well aired, night and day, and should be devoted to the exclusive use of the child.

These children should never be allowed to sit on the floor. It is always a difficult matter to avoid this, but it must be religiously guarded against; otherwise a cold is the inevitable result.

A change of air is sometimes advisable and essential, especially during the hot, humid weather of July and August. Much better results will be obtained by sending these children to the mountains than to the seashore.

Delicate children should always be clothed warmly, but not too warmly. The feet and legs must always be kept comfortable. Moderate exercise, short of fatigue, is necessary. A midday nap after the noon meal should be taken every day. The child should be undressed and put to bed for two hours and left there, whether it sleeps or not. This applies to delicate children of all ages.

The education of delicate children should be postponed until the health is restored. They should, however, be made to obey and they should be taught good habits. When school work begins it should be made light and easy. They should not go to school before the eighth year, and then not unless physically fit. They should not play at rough games or with rough companions, though it is not wise to shield them too much. Their habits and peculiarities should be studied and every possible effort made to direct them kindly and wisely so that they may contribute to their own upbuilding.

A systematic observance of these suggestions will save many lives and will aid very considerably in producing stronger men and women. Infinite patience, tact and self-sacrifice is necessary, but the results in every case justify the measures adopted.[Pg 286]

Indiscriminate Feeding: Poor Appetite.—In considering many of the diseases of childhood the term "indiscriminate feeding" is used. An explanation of just what is meant by this will be of decided advantage. There are two fundamental essentials in the successful feeding of infants and children: regularity and suitable food.

A child whose feeding intervals are not regular and whose food is unsuitable is a victim of indiscriminate feeding.

The lack of observance of the regularity rule always leads to loss of appetite and indigestion.

Loss of appetite is a serious condition in a growing child and may give infinite trouble. Indigestion in a growing child is unnecessary, unfortunate, and frequently is the one factor that spoils an entire life. It is unnecessary, because it means and is caused by neglect on the part of the mother; it is unfortunate, because it always paves the way for any serious ailment that is epidemic or "in the air"; and it is important, because it very frequently weakens the stomach and renders it unfit for normal digestion for a long period, if not for life.

If for some reason a child's appetite becomes poor and it is not properly managed until the appetite is restored to normal, indiscriminate feeding is always the result.

The reason for the poor appetite may be because the child is kept indoors too long, or because it is being fed on unsuitable food, or is living in unsanitary surroundings, or many other reasons, sometimes trifling reasons, may cause it. When a child will not eat at meal time, the mother feels that it should eat sometime, so she encourages it to eat between meals, and because of a mistaken kindness she breaks the law of regularity,—a law that can never be broken without serious results following. A child in this condition becomes a disturber of the peace; the parents can do nothing with him; he insists on eating just what he likes and when he likes; and he chooses, as a rule, candy, cake, pastries, ice cream, tea, coffee. Indigestion follows, the child loses weight, is languid and listless and constipated.[Pg 287]

When finally the physician is called in he finds it necessary to go back to first principles. He lays down the law in a definite, stern way, and the mother and the child must obey. Most parents know and admit they are doing wrong to give in to a whimsical child, and if they would only make up their minds to conquer when conquering is easy they would save themselves many heartaches, many regrets, and the child much suffering and much possible permanent injury as a consequence. Usually one parent is willing to be master but the other lacks the mental equipment to meet the issue, and argues, as he or she imagines, in favor of the child. The parent whose instinct is correct, whose judgment is true, whose interpretation of the situation is just, should not be dissuaded, or argued away from his or her duty. If it is the first real problem in your domestic experience in which a decided stand must be made, make it without fear and without hesitation, and carry it through to the bitter end. Results will justify and vindicate you.

The general treatment of these children will be found outlined in the following paragraph on Loss of Appetite.

Loss of Appetite.—If a child complains of not being hungry, and will not take enough food, and if this condition continues for some time, we must regard the matter as being abnormal and find the cause. This is necessary because a child must eat in order to maintain a certain standard of growth and vitality. These children are not sick; they are active and continue to play as usual and they sleep soundly, but they have no appetite. One of the most frequent causes of this condition is too frequent feedings. Some children are naturally small eaters. They thrive and maintain a satisfactory weight; their system seems not to demand large quantities or even ordinary quantities of food. Parents observe this habit of little eating and begin to coax and bribe the child to eat more at meal time, and to eat between meals. In this way the child really overeats, the appetite becomes capricious, and the stomach rebels. In a very short time the condition of "loss of appetite" is established as a consequence. Another cause is the[Pg 288] drinking of too much milk, and yet another and very common cause is indiscriminate eating of candy, cakes crackers, and fruit between meals. Children who are fed at the table with adults eat things they should not eat, and spoil their digestive organs and loss of appetite is the result. The Scotch custom of compelling children to eat at a separate table is an excellent one. They are not tempted to ask for things they cannot have. Lack of fresh air and exercise frequently results in impaired appetite.

Treatment.—The very first thing to do with these children is to stop any habit that may be responsible for the loss of appetite. If the child has been eating between meals, stop it absolutely. If too much milk has been taken, stop milk entirely. If the child has not been getting enough fresh air, or if it has been sleeping in a badly ventilated room, or if baths have been too infrequent, rectify the fault. If eating at the family table and fed indiscriminately, change the programme; feed him before the family sits down to meals. Now regulate the time of feeding to suit the age of the child and adhere to strict regularity. It is a pernicious and absolutely wrong custom to force children to eat, or to coax them to eat when they do not want to eat. Loss of appetite will never be cured by forced feeding, or by reducing the interval between feedings, or by giving the child stronger or more concentrated food under the mistaken idea that in this way the loss of appetite can be "made up." The interval of feeding should rather be lengthened than otherwise in order to give the digestive organs an opportunity to regain the normal desire for food. Pay strict attention to the bowels. Be certain the child has a daily satisfactory movement and that he drinks frequently between meals.

If the child does not promptly respond to the proper hygienic and dietary treatment as outlined above there are two things that can be done:

1st: Send the child away. A change of scene and climate will sometimes work like a charm in these cases, and will, after a reasonable length of time, establish a permanently good appetite.[Pg 289]

2nd: If this is not possible, as sometimes it may not be with poor patients, then we can give the child suitable tonics.

Overeating.—The large majority of individuals eat too much. Most of us would enjoy better health, better spirits, and greater efficiency if we consumed from one-third to one-half less food than we habitually do.

Every living organism requires a certain amount of nourishment according to the work performed and to replenish wear and tear; when food is supplied in excess, the system cannot utilize it, but it is compelled to rid itself of the excess in some way. The work involved in this eliminating process is exceedingly detrimental to the various organs and to the individual. To overeat is to overwork, and to overwork a machine or an animal is not only poor economy but bad judgment. If the digestive apparatus is required to work overtime, it is a self-evident assumption that the various organs will not digest efficiently the food necessary for ordinary existence. If the necessary nourishment is not adequately digested, the general health will suffer as a consequence. If the general health is below standard the individual will not be competent to carry on the requirements of a normal, healthy life.

We must, however, give some thought to the effect which the excess of food exerts upon the human machine.

Nature provides and maintains a standard relationship between the capacity of the individual and his needs. A child has a digestive capacity to digest and assimilate a quantity of food sufficient for his growth and proper nourishment; an adult maintains the same standard according to his requirements. All the other organs are adjusted to harmonize with this scheme. If we overeat, the immediate result is to disorganize this relationship between the various organs; hence we have a multitude of effects which manifest themselves in various ways as a direct result of overeating. The combined general effect expresses itself in the form of what is regarded as poor health and a low standard of efficiency. When a larger quantity of food is taken into the stomach than[Pg 290] it can properly digest within a reasonable time, two conditions immediately follow. The stomach itself is dilated and the food is not thoroughly digested. If the habit is persisted in, indigestion, and later chronic gastritis ensues. The direct symptoms of these conditions are given in detail in another part of this book. Very few individuals, however, appreciate the indirect consequences of overeating and of indiscriminate eating on the general health. It is impossible to tabulate in so many words the effect which this habit has on efficiency and temperament. We read and hear a great deal to-day about efficiency. Now, an individual's efficiency is an expression of that individual's health standard or capacity. To be 100 per cent. efficient one must enjoy good health. It would be absurd to expect a high standard of efficiency from an individual with a low standard of health. Poor health means poor vitality. Vitality is the mark of the master. Without vitality one can never dominate. All the great achievements of the race have been consummated by those who conserved their vitality. No single factor contributes a larger percentage of inefficients and failures than overeating. The man or woman who, from habit or experience, has learned the lesson of right eating and living need not be lacking in efficiency, nor need they despair of the attainment of success.

Symptoms of Overeating.—Efficiency depends not only upon one's capacity to perform, but upon the character of the performance. The spirit must be willing to perform. The overeater is heavy, phlegmatic, indifferent, lacking in energy, tact and initiative. She is constantly subjecting her system to needless overwork; she is depressed, nervous, imaginative and she is not ambitious. She is a victim of self-poisoning, of constipation, indigestion, headaches, flatulency, neuralgia, vertigo, and melancholia. An overeater never enjoys good health, never is efficient, and cannot possibly be successful.

To enjoy good health one should know how to select food and how to combine and proportion it. It has been said that the American people are a race of dyspeptics,[Pg 291] and it must be admitted that the assertion is more or less true. There are millions of people who suffer from indigestion in some degree, and it may justly be said that indigestion has its beginning in overeating, in some form. It may not be overeating in actual bulk, but it is overeating some article or articles that do not agree with the individual, and the fact that certain articles do not agree is unquestionably dependent upon the nervous temperament of the American people—and the temperament of a people is a product of the kind of existence the people subject themselves to. We are, therefore, unwittingly, victims of our environment.

Correct eating means simple eating—only a few things at a time. Food should be selected according to one's age and occupation, and according to the season of the year. To eat habitually large quantities and at the same time a large variety is suicide pure and simple. If one dared to make the experiment of cutting down one's diet one-half, it is absolutely certain the effect would be immediate benefit. The benefit would not only be manifest in the physical betterment, but the efficiency and general well-being would be greatly enhanced. It is not the kind of food that makes a dyspeptic, but the quantity. A well person need not consider whether a certain kind of food will or will not agree, providing she does not eat too freely of that food, or combine it with other food. The combination of which may in itself form too much of one kind at a time.

Some people imagine, for example, that oatmeal porridge does not agree with them. When the matter is inquired into, however, it is found that they habitually eat bread, eggs, and other articles, with coffee at the the same meal with the porridge. From this combination they experience distress and blame the porridge. If these would take a plate of oatmeal porridge with cream and salt, and some stewed fruit for breakfast they would not experience any trouble, and this would be an ample meal for the ordinary individual. It is not the porridge, but the unsuitable combination, that is at fault. The same may be said of milk. Many people state that they cannot take milk and they deprive themselves[Pg 292] of one of the very best articles of diet because of this idea. There are very few people in the world who cannot take milk in some way. It is not the milk that is at fault; it is the combination of it with other less nutritious articles that is the cause of the distress. Even candy is responsible for thousands of cases of indigestion. Anyone may safely take a reasonable quantity of good candy, but if it is taken at a wrong time, or combined with other articles, it may readily produce indigestion.

Indiscriminate eating and overeating are prolific causes of rheumatism, kidney disease, heart disease, liver troubles, obesity, arteriosclerosis, and apoplexy. These diseases are notoriously on the increase and must be construed as a direct consequence of the tendency of the American people to overeat and to eat indiscriminately.

Bran as a Food.—In the chapter on constipation there may be found a formula for making bran muffins. These muffins are invaluable to children in health, and to the victim of indigestion or constipation, whether child or adult. One muffin with each meal will solve the problem of constipation in growing children without the use of drugs or other aid. They will regulate the bowels of adults in many instances without resorting to drugs.

Raw fruit in season, or stewed fruit, or a baked apple, with a light boiled egg and one bran muffin, is an ample and a nourishing breakfast for a child at school.

For lunch the same child should have a plate of thoroughly done vegetable soup, a bran muffin, and more fruit. After school, a glass of milk with two or three Graham wafers may be given.

For dinner the child at school may have a mixed meal. This meal should not be later than six-thirty o'clock and the child should retire at eight-thirty at the latest. A bran muffin should be taken with this meal unless the child's bowels are too loose.

Mothers should insist on their children eating these muffins. If a child eats only what it likes it will not eat what is good for it. If the mother insists in the right way she will win; if she does not the child will win. If the child wins, the mother is the wrong kind of mother. I do not know of any other single article of diet that[Pg 293] is of such value to growing children as these bran muffins. Children who eat them regularly will have less sickness than other children; they will be strong, healthy and full of energy. The bran in itself is not responsible for this list of excellent acquirements, but the regular eating of the bran is. Most ailments of children are of gastro-intestinal origin; bran keeps the entire length of the gastro-intestinal tract sweet and clean; if the child eats a bran muffin with each meal it will not have much desire or much room for any other form of bread or pastry. If white bread or pastry is abstained from the child will not have indigestion, or constipation, and hence it will not be constantly poisoning itself as most children do whose diet is not restricted and whose bowels are more or less constipated.

These muffins should be made of the ordinary unsifted bran. If this is not procurable the sifted bran (Johnstone's) may be employed. This bran may be bought in any good grocery.

Modern milling methods, modern cookery, and modern methods of forced farming, have each contributed their share of rendering food inert and frequently deleterious. The miller has extracted the coarse cellulose from the various flours in the effort to manufacture a product suitable to the super-civilized public demand. This cellulose is absolutely essential to gastric and intestinal digestion, and if children are deprived of it constipation and indigestion are the natural result. Forced farming accomplishes the same effect—the fiber of the vegetable is deficient. Bran is rich in mineral salts, iron, protein, and phosphates, and gives to growing children the ingredients which ordinary food is deficient in. Bran prevents intestinal fermentation and children who eat it are free from intestinal gas and putrefaction. It harmonizes chemically with all other foods. Children should be made to take it every day as a matter of self-preservation and of duty.

Hysterical Children.—Hysteria is not a disease of infancy or of young children. It is seen as a rule after the eight year. Male as well as female children may be the victims to an equal degree. It is much more[Pg 294] frequently seen in the offspring of parents who are themselves nervous, or alcoholic, or who suffer from insanity, or have insanity in the family history. If these children in addition to the hereditary influence suffer from stomach or intestinal disease, or general poor health and are overworked at school, they are very apt to become hysterical.

They are capricious, indifferent, and excitable. Their disposition is irritable; they frequently exhibit fits of great excitability of temper and passion. They cry or weep without cause. They often have hallucinations and while asleep have attacks resembling night terrors. They complain of pains in the joints, and are frequently treated for disease that does not exist. Such condition as hysterical cough, spasm of the muscles of the face, mouth, eyes, and of the neck exist and are difficult to diagnose from real disease. These children complain of painful sensations and sensitive areas and exaggerate all symptoms unnecessarily.

The possibility of curing these patients is good, providing the treatment is faithfully carried out. It is less favorable when marked hereditary influences are strong.

Treatment.—In all children of distinctly nervous type and especially those of nervous parents, the first essential duty is to develop their muscular system. Try in every way to make healthy animals of them. Attention and treatment should not be directed toward the nervous system. If the child is made strong by out-door life, good plain, digestible food, early hours, regular sleep in thoroughly aired rooms, regular bathing, and if the school work is conducted with moderation and judgment, the nerves and the nervous temperament will participate in the healthy growth which will follow as a result. Tea and coffee should be forbidden. Exciting books and questionable entertainment as given in picture shows and theaters must not be allowed. If older members of the family, or parents, are excitable and nervous the children should be sent away to the country from them.

They should be put in charge of a person who will exercise firm control over them. It may be necessary[Pg 295] to take these patients away from other children, and isolate them under proper control until they are able to control themselves. They should be interested in exercise that compels them to work; they should live and if convenient sleep out of doors; and they should take iron or cod liver oil, or any other indicated tonic. If they complain of pain they should receive cold-water douches, or the cold pack, or the shower bath; and they should be put to bed and treated firmly but kindly. Attention to the bowels is always essential, because these children are as a rule the victims of chronic constipation.

What a Mother Should Know About Cathartics and How to Give a Child a Dose of Castor Oil.—Broadly speaking there are three kinds of cathartics. I will, in a simple way, explain their action so that a mother may know which one to select under certain circumstances. Frequently a mother is told by her physician to "keep the bowels of her child open." Few mothers know how to keep the bowels open, and as this is an important matter, every mother should know the reason why "any" laxative or cathartic is not always suitable.

Castor Oil.—This is one of the oldest and one of the best cathartics we possess for children. It is a mechanical cathartic; it acts in exactly the same way as a street-cleaning machine. It cleans the street by sweeping or pushing everything before it.

Calomel—This is a chemical cathartic. It acts through the blood. When it is absorbed by the blood its chemical ingredients act on certain nerves as irritants. These nerves excite the liver and bowel to action and an evacuation is the result.

Citrate of Magnesia.—This is a saline laxative. It acts by drawing out of the bowel wall enough liquid from the blood to sweep the contents out. It may be likened to the street cleaner who flushes and cleans the street by means of a hose pipe attached to the water hydrant.

Under what condition should a mother use these remedies? Castor oil is ordinarily the best cathartic in childhood; it is not, however, always the best. Most ailments[Pg 296] of children are of gastro-intestinal origin—they have either overeaten or they have eaten the wrong kind of food. The stomach and bowel are overloaded: they must be cleaned out. We want a mechanical cathartic, one that will push everything ahead of it, so we use castor oil. When a child needs a cleaning out, use castor oil. By a "cleaning out" we mean, when we know he has eaten too much of a questionable variety of food, as pastries, cakes, fruit, ice cream, etc., as children do at parties; or when he has eaten unripe fruit, as green apples, etc.; or when for some reason he is constipated and complains of not feeling well, use castor oil.

If you decide to use castor oil, use enough. A large dose will act promptly and with less pain and with more certain results than a small dose.

It is always safe and it is always best to decide upon castor oil as the proper remedy, if the child has no fever. If he has a fever he will most likely vomit castor oil when another kind of cathartic would stay on the stomach.

Castor oil works more effectively, more thoroughly, and is less likely to be vomited if given on an empty stomach, so we give it two hours after eating and we give no food for two hours after it is taken.

Castor oil is distinctly of advantage in many chronic diseases of the intestines because of its healing properties. In chronic colitis, for example, when the child is suffering with malnutrition, irregular bowel action with an odor, and mucous or bloody stools, a combination of castor oil and salol, in emulsion, in small doses,—to which a small quantity of opium may be added or withheld according to the frequency of the movements,—with an occasional colon irrigation, is sometimes invaluable.

Mothers must remember that castor oil is not good in the treatment of constipation, because its after effect is to constipate, consequently we would not use it "to keep the bowels open,"—it is only of use to clean the bowel out thoroughly when that is indicated.

How to Give a Dose of Castor Oil—The best way to give a child castor oil is as follows: Place the bottle containing the oil on its side on a piece of ice in the ice box; chill it thoroughly. Take a tablespoon and smear[Pg 297] it with butter; pour the ice cold oil into the spoon; it will stick together like a piece of chewing gum and it will slide out of the buttered spoon in one lump. In this way it will not spread over the mouth and teeth and throat, leaving a bad taste, but will go straight and surely into the stomach. The child cannot swallow some and retain enough in the mouth to sputter it all over itself and only get half a dose; it will not nauseate it, because it practically is tasteless if given cold, and the stomach will tolerate the cold oil much better than when given in the ordinary way.

A baby can be given oil in the same way, but in smaller doses. When the teaspoon is put into the mouth of a baby it should be immediately turned on its side so that it will keep the mouth open. If the nose is held closed and the mouth wide open for a few seconds the baby cannot spit the oil out—it must swallow, and if the oil sticks together as cold oil will, it gets the whole dose. It usually takes two persons to give a baby a dose of oil— one to open the mouth and give the medicine, the other to hold the nose and arms.

Calomel.—The general indication for calomel is fever. When a child develops a disease it immediately gets a temperature, and very frequently the fever is quite high because the slightest ailment gives a child fever. When fever begins, digestion practically stops, it is therefore imperative to clean the whole gastro-intestinal canal; otherwise the undigested material will putrefy and poison the entire system and render the disease more serious than it need be.

Now we select in such conditions calomel for two reasons:

First, because the presence of fever indicates that infection of the blood is taking place; this may come either from the intestinal canal itself, or from the germs of the disease with which the child is suffering. Since calomel acts chemically through the blood it is the cathartic indicated.

Second, because a cathartic like castor oil does not act through the blood and it would most likely be vomited by a fevered stomach.[Pg 298]

Certain conditions indicate calomel; biliousness and jaundice, for example, because it has a specific action on the liver and if the liver is at fault calomel is the proper remedy.

Calomel is best given in small divided doses, 1-10 of a grain every half hour, for ten doses. It is best given combined with soda; every drug store carries tablets of calomel and soda for this reason.

Calomel should never be given in the treatment of constipation, nor should it be used indiscriminately by mothers, as much harm may result. It has its specific use as indicated above, but it should never be used under any other circumstances.

Citrate of Magnesia.—This is a mild laxative. After the bowels have been thoroughly opened with castor oil or calomel, small doses of citrate of magnesia may be given for a few days, "to keep the bowels open." There is no danger or harm in its use if used for this purpose. It must not be used, however, in the treatment of constipation of children for the simple reason that you cannot cure constipation by the use of drugs of any kind. Laxatives of this type have become a national curse. Adults, especially women, use them constantly. All these advertised saline laxative waters work by weakening the blood—when a dose is taken the chemicals in it draw through the bowel wall blood serum, and produce, because of the excess of this watery fluid, large, and frequently many, liquid movements.

If this practice is continued, as it often is every day, the quality of the blood will suffer seriously, and many individuals are the victims of neuralgic pains, headaches, nervousness, insomnia, anemia, and general broken health as a direct consequence of this pernicious habit.

Mothers will try to remember, therefore, that drugs and saline waters have no place in the treatment of constipation in children or themselves. Constipation must be treated by diet, exercise regular living and by the observance of hygienic and sanitary common-sense rules.[Pg 299]

VACCINATION

Time for Vaccination.—The best time to vaccinate a child is during the first three months if he is healthy. The reason for selecting so early a period is because the constitutional disturbances are much less at this time than in later childhood. It should not be done during active dentition. If the child is delicate if his nutrition is bad it should be deferred until a later time. Children suffering from eczema or from any skin disease or those syphilitic should not be vaccinated until it is compulsory, or until exposed to small-pox.

Methods of Vaccinating.—It is customary in America to vaccinate at one point rather than to make a number of inoculations as is the custom in some other countries. The leg or the arm is the usual location selected. In infants the sore can be protected better on the leg; in children of the run-about age, the arm is the better location because it can be kept at rest easier.

Before vaccinating the skin should be rendered surgically clean; this can be done by washing with soap and water, drying and then rubbing with alcohol. The wound should be left uncovered for about twenty minutes to dry, it may then be covered with a bandage, or with a vaccine shield. The part should not be washed for twenty-four hours.

The Symptoms of Successful Vaccination.—Nothing is noticed until the third or fourth day, when a red papule appears. In the course of the following day a vesicle appears; this vesicle enlarges until it reaches its full development on the ninth day. The size of the vesicle is about one-half inch in diameter; it is surrounded with a reddish inflammatory area for about two inches. The vesicle begins to dry and is shortly a dark crust which remains from one to three weeks and then falls off. It leaves a bluish scar which soon turns white and the part is roughened and honeycombed. During the period when the vaccination is at its height the child suffers from fever and irritability and loss of appetite.

If vaccination does not "take" in an infant it should be done two or three times and if then unsuccessful it[Pg 300] should be repeated every year until it takes. The fact that vaccination does not take does not imply that the child would not take small-pox but rather that the vaccine used is not suitable. There are some children, however, who seem to be immune to vaccination.

Sometimes the symptoms are more severe than those enumerated; this seems to depend upon the susceptibility of the child. The vesicle may be much larger and the area of inflammation much more dense and angry. The fever may be higher and may last longer; there may be a general rash and the degree of depression more profound. Vesicles may be produced on other parts of the body as a result of scratching. Mothers must always remember that vaccination is a surgical wound to begin with and that it is capable of infection in the same way as are other wounds, and that any result coming from such an infection is not due to the vaccine or to the process of vaccination, but to the infection. Many people get unjust ideas about vaccination from just such cases. If the mother is not cleanly or neglects the vaccinated area and permits it to become infected she must not and others should not decry vaccination as a consequence. Anyone who doubts the virtue of vaccination is condemning himself; he is simply ignorant of the accumulation of evidence in favor of it and assumes a position without any possible justification. The mortality of vaccination is stated by Voigt from statistics to be 35 in 2,275,000 cases. In fact, all the deaths are from causes which are preventable and no doubt the result of direct carelessness on the part of the operator or the mother.

Treatment.—The mother must understand in what way she may contribute to the successful termination of a case of vaccination. She should see that the part upon which the child is to be vaccinated is absolutely clean so far as she can make it with soap and water. She should see that the part is allowed to dry thoroughly after vaccination. She should not wash the part for at least twenty-four hours. If a vaccine shield is put on she should not disturb it. If the mother is prepared to do her part faithfully a vaccine shield is not necessary from a medical standpoint and in some cases it is[Pg 301] objectionable. A simple, clean bandage is all that is necessary. It is very important that the child be kept from scratching the part; most of the troubles of vaccination come from this habit. It is desirable that the limb should be kept at rest during the stage when the process is at its height. If the vesicle discharges it is necessary that the area should be kept clean and dusted with boracic acid. If the wound becomes infected it must be treated by a physician. The mother must not resort to home remedies in such cases unless she is prepared to take the consequences, which may be serious.

[Pg 303]

CHAPTER XXII

CONSTIPATION IN INFANTS AND CHILDREN

"It is a greater disgrace to be sick than to be in the penitentiary. When you are arrested it is because you have broken a man-made statute, but when you are ill, it is because you have disobeyed one of God's laws."

Constipation—Regularity of Bowel Function—The Function of the Stomach—Fermentation—Incomplete Constipation—Importance of a Clean Bowel—A Daily Movement of the Bowel Necessary—Constipation in Breast-Fed Infants—Treatment of Constipation in Breast-Fed Infants—Constipation in Bottle-Fed Infants—Treatment of Constipation in Bottle-Fed Infants—Constipation in Children Over Two Years of Age—Diet List for Constipation in Children—Bran Muffins in Constipation—Treatment of Obstinate Constipation—Oil Injections in Constipation.

CONSTIPATION. REGULARITY OF BOWEL FUNCTION

The most frequent cause of ill health and inefficiency in the human race is inattention to regulation of the bowel function. Good health depends upon many causes of which good blood is an absolutely necessary requisite. Good blood depends upon what feeds and sustains it. There are other contributing factors, such as the proper kind of exercise, the proper amount and quality of fresh air, the method of living, etc., but these are all food in a sense. The food we take in is acted upon by the various digestive juices until everything is extracted from it that contributes to the building up of the body. Whatever is left, whatever the body does not want, is immediately, or within a reasonable time, passed out in the form of a movement of the bowels.

If any part of the digestive function is deficient, impaired health, or mental and physical inefficiency expressed in the form of indigestion, is the result. If[Pg 304] the bowel is at fault, constipation is the usual consequence. A perfectly healthy living machine must maintain a perfect digestion and regular bowel movements.

The Function of the Stomach is to mix and churn the food, and to add certain ingredients to the mixture so that before it is carried into the intestines it is (as far as it is the stomach's duty to render it) ready to be absorbed into the system. Before it reaches that part of the intestine which absorbs, it is acted upon again and certain other ingredients are added to it by certain other digestive organs. In time it is in shape to be used and it is sent along on its way. As it passes onward the little sucking glands in the wall of the bowel suck up all the liquid element in the mass of food. The liquid element in the mass is the food itself, rendered liquid by the stomach and other digestive organs and juices. The remaining solid mass is that part of the food which the body cannot use and does not want. By the time the liquid element is absorbed, the solid mass (always kept moving by the bowel wall) has reached the rectum, ready to be passed out at once, or very soon, provided—and upon this provision depends the success of the entire process,—it has all been done within a certain time. If the stomach takes too long to do its work we have indigestion. If the bowel takes too long to do its work we have constipation.

Fermentation.—Now let us consider the matter from another standpoint. If food stays too long in the stomach it begins to ferment. When anything ferments it makes and evolves gas. You, no doubt, have noticed many times how the cork pops out of a bottle if its contents are "working," or fermenting. If you watch that bottle you will notice that it is quietly or actively evolving air bubbles. That is gas,—gas manufactured by the process of fermentation. This is exactly the process that goes on in the stomach or bowel of a dyspeptic, and it is this collection of foul, poisonous gas that causes the distress and bloated feeling which every dyspeptic suffers from after eating,—if it is this "flatulent" type of indigestion which is present.

The Significance of Constipation.—If the food takes[Pg 305] too long to pass through the bowel it causes, as we have stated, constipation. What is the real significance of constipation? It means that in passing through the bowel the food has given up all its liquid element (which is all its nourishing element), but the bowel has been too slow in passing it along. Consequently it is not ready to be expelled while it is yet a harmless semi-solid mass. It stays in the bowel too long—it begins to putrefy, bacteria attack it, and it is soon a semi-liquid, foul, rotting mass. The sucking glands in the intestinal wall continue to suck—that is their duty. They cannot discriminate between what is good and what is bad—they simply go on absorbing whatever is there to absorb. So there are absorbed into the system liquid and gaseous products which are poison.

This process has been called by a number of names; "self-poisoning" explains the condition thoroughly. The other names are, auto-infection, auto-intoxication, enteric-infection, enteric-toxemia, intestinal indigestion.

The condition is a serious one, because it is absolutely impossible to feel well, or to enjoy good health, while it lasts. The feeling of being constantly sick, yet not sick enough to stop working or to demand a radical cure, affects a woman's efficiency, interferes with her capacity to work, her ability to render the home an abode of contentment, to be an agreeable companion, or to adequately take care of her children.

The constant absorption of intestinal poisons affects the system itself,—the symptoms are headache, neuralgia, loss of appetite, nervousness, insomnia, vertigo, inability to concentrate, lassitude, indigestion. The condition which we name constipation is therefore one of supreme importance. From a medical standpoint, it is the biggest problem in the whole realm of disease. It is the most significant hygienic function of life, and it is becoming more and more important, and more and more a problem. Every modern factor upon which physical efficiency seems to depend is an enemy to the systematic regulation of this function. Our method of hurried and indiscriminate eating, our system of strenuous living, our unsanitary environment, our business activity, our method of pursuing[Pg 306] pleasure, take no account of, and resent the time devoted to cultivating, as a hygienic necessity, this toilet requirement. This imperative call of nature is pushed aside by the child at play, by the housewife for a duty which could wait, by the merchant for an engagement. It is particularly an American disease, and it is uniquely an American woman's affliction. It is a curious commentary on the intelligence of the American people, who are ordinarily alert and analytical, to realize how few of them really know how serious a matter constipation is. They don't know because they have given the matter absolutely no thought. They have accepted it as a mere matter of fact, almost of fate.

Incomplete Constipation.—There is a type of constipation that is not known to the average person and not well understood by those few who know of its existence. In this form of constipation there is a daily bowel movement but the movement is not complete. The bowel does not thoroughly empty itself; it has established this habit because of conditions under which it has had to do its work. If a woman neglects herself, becomes muscularly inactive, does not take proper out-door exercise, grows fat and lazy, eats irregularly and indiscriminately,—the bowel suffers with the rest of the system. The woman may have a healthy appetite, may eat the wrong things at the wrong time, yet the bowel is supposed to go on acting rightly, but it does not. It, too, becomes lazy and acquires bad habits, and this form of incomplete constipation is the result. These patients look healthy and get little sympathy for any pains they may have. They may even gain in weight; they get headaches once in a while, and if they go shopping or visiting they don't feel quite well afterward. They are suffering from the effects of chronic constipation, though their bowels are apparently regular. They are marching onward toward apoplexy or Bright's disease of the kidney.

Importance of a Clean Bowel.—Every mother, sooner or later, observes that a physician always thoroughly cleans out the bowel of a sick child at once, no matter what the character of the sickness is. He does this for two reasons,—first, because he knows that the great[Pg 307] majority of children's ailments are of gastro-intestinal origin; second, if the origin of the disease is not in the stomach or bowels, experience has taught him that if the bowels are clean at the beginning of a disease, that disease will run a milder and shorter course than if complicated with a condition of self-poisoning. If a child develops fever the digestive function stops; whatever food is in the stomach or bowel will promptly ferment and putrefy because of the abnormal heat caused by the fever and the arrested digestion. If this is not cleaned out at once the self-poisoning process begins.

The above is a suggestive admission for a physician to make. It simply means that the vast majority of the calls made by a physician on ailing children are caused by errors in diet and can be completely cured by a dose of castor oil or calomel, or, better still, need never occur.

A mother who neglects, who is guilty of inattention to the conditions of her child's bowel, fails in one of the most important duties of motherhood. I know as a father and a physician that if a child's bowel acts regularly and thoroughly, that child is fortified to the highest efficient degree against the multitude of little ailments common to all children. A clean bowel means good blood, good digestion, ability to exercise properly, to sleep soundly and to think clearly. Such a child will resist infection and throw off the minor troubles that pave the way for serious sickness. It is a secret worth knowing.

A Daily Movement of the Bowel Necessary.—In order to preserve good health one thorough movement of the bowel is necessary daily. A baby may have two or three and enjoy robust health. A larger daily number suggests an abnormal condition of the bowel and an investigation should be made. If a nursing baby's bowels do not move before bedtime it should be given an injection of equal parts of glycerine and hot water, one-half cupful; or an enema of soap and water, or a glycerine suppository. When a child is six months old, in some sooner, it should be put on the stool at a certain time every morning. This will aid in the establishment of the habit, as a child soon understands why it is made to assume this position and acts accordingly.[Pg 308]

The condition referred to above and which we termed incomplete constipation may affect the nursing infant. A child's bowels may move daily and yet the child will suffer from constipation. If the movements are watched it will be observed that certain children strain when at stool, and after a time succeed in passing hard, dry lumps or balls of fecal matter. Such a movement is a certain indication that the bowel is not emptying itself satisfactorily and that a constant toxemia or poisoning is going on. Very faithful efforts should be made to remedy this condition by the use of articles of diet that are known to be laxative, otherwise the condition is one that will "grow" with the child and establish an obstinate chronic constipation with all its miseries and dangers.

Constipation in Breast-Fed Infants.—Many nursing infants thrive and gain in weight, yet they are constipated. Before you drug your baby be sure the fault is not your own. Many mothers are responsible for the constipation with which baby suffers. If the mother is constipated, so will the child be. Cure the constipation of the mother and the baby's bowels will regulate themselves. Nursing mothers who are large tea-drinkers have irregular bowels as a rule. A baby whose mother is lazy or indolent, who does not take a reasonable amount of exercise, whose diet is faulty and whose hours are bad, is a sufferer from constipation. The mother's life must be regulated, her diet and habits corrected, and the instructions carried out as already recommended. The breast milk should be examined and if any cause for constipation exists in it, it should be rectified as suggested elsewhere.

If it is thought advisable to resort to drugs for the immediate relief of the constipation of infants, the best ones are the aromatic fluid extract of cascara sagrada; milk of magnesia with equal parts of the aromatic syrup of rhubarb given in doses of one to three teaspoonfuls daily.

Irrigations, enemas, and suppositories should not be used continuously. The habit is a bad one. The parts become accustomed to their use and fail to act. If the child is passing dry and hard stools it is of advantage to inject two ounces of warm sweet oil at night, allowing[Pg 309] it to remain in the bowel until the following morning. See page 312.

Constipation in Bottle-Fed Infants.—It is much easier to treat the constipation of bottle-fed babies than of those breast-fed, because the food can be changed to ensure regular bowel movements. The first change to be made in a bottle-fed baby who is habitually constipated is to add more cream to the food. The way to do this is to take out of the bottle of each feeding one tablespoonful of the food and put in its place one tablespoonful pure cream. If this change partly rectifies the bowel ailment, add more cream until the bowels are of the proper consistency. Milk given constipated babies should be raw, never boiled, as boiled milk will always aggravate the trouble.

The use of oatmeal water instead of plain water in making the baby's food may cure the bowel trouble. Taking the sugar of milk out of the baby's food and putting in its place the same quantity of Mellin's food will sometimes cure the constipation.

One or two teaspoonfuls of milk of magnesia put into one feeding daily, or fifteen drops to one tablespoonful of the aromatic fluid extract of cascara sagrada will move the bowels. Orange juice, strained, two teaspoonfuls twice daily, is an excellent remedy and should be tried in every case. Sweet oil and pure cod liver oil, in doses of thirty drops to two teaspoonfuls three times daily after feedings, if the little patient is poorly nourished. If the stools remain hard and dry, an injection of two ounces of warm sweet oil at bedtime is an excellent method of aiding the bowel. The oil should remain in the bowel all night. This lubricates the parts, softens the fecal mass and stimulates the gut to perform its own work. See page 312.

Constipation in Children Over Two Years of Age.—Most children when put upon a varied diet after the nursing days are over are relieved of any constipation which may have existed up to that time. There are a few, however, whose condition does not seem to improve. These children need attention. We should first insist on regular habits. A child should be told that its[Pg 310] bowels must move every morning after breakfast. If this is absolutely insisted upon the child will soon recognize the uselessness of fighting the proposition and submit. If at any time a conscientious effort is made to move the bowel without result after fifteen minutes it is wise to use a glycerine suppository so that the bowel will empty itself.

It has been stated in another part of this book that there are children with whom milk does not agree. Experience has taught us that milk, especially milk that has been boiled, causes more cases of constipation in growing children than all other causes combined. Find out if it is milk that is the cause in any individual case. While these children cannot take whole milk just as it comes from the dairy without suffering in a great many ways, they can take milk and water, or milk and oatmeal water, prepared in the following way, without becoming constipated. A bottle of fresh milk is allowed to stand in a cool place for five hours, when the top ten ounces are skimmed off with a Chapin dipper and mixed with twelve ounces of oatmeal gruel or plain water. This can be used as a drink.

Parents can select from the following list of articles such combinations as may be suitable to constitute the regular meals of a constipated child:

Lamb chops. Rare steak. Rare roast beef. Hashed chicken. Soft boiled eggs. Cracked wheat. Hominy. Cornmeal. Oatmeal, Scotch. Bran biscuits. Oatmeal crackers. Graham wafers. Stewed or baked apple. Apple sauce. Plain vanilla ice cream. Animal broths, purées of peas. Beans, and lentils. Peas. String beans. Spinach. Cauliflower. Asparagus. Stewed tomatoes, strained. Whole wheat bread. Zwieback. Custard. Stewed prunes. Junket. Cornstarch.

Malted milk is agreeable and advisable as a drink.

Orange juice or a scraped raw apple is allowable at this time. Constipated children should eat plenty[Pg 311] of good butter. Olive oil, two or three teaspoonfuls after each meal, is excellent. It can be kept up for months to advantage. Older children may eat raw and cooked fruits, figs, dates, baked potatoes, poultry, and fish. One or two raw apples or a peach or orange may be given daily. A strict observance of the above rules and diet will result in normal movements of the bowel if persisted in for a reasonable time. It may be necessary occasionally to use a suppository or an enema now and again until the habit is established.

In children from five to fifteen years of age the use of bran muffins, with fruit, etc., as described above, will effect a cure of constipation without having to resort to drugs. I have cured many cases of constipation in growing children with these muffins without making any other change in their diet or habits.

RECIPE FOR BRAN MUFFINS

Take one pint of best flour, one quart unsifted bran, one teaspoonful bicarbonate of soda (baking soda), a pinch of salt.

Mix these thoroughly together, then add: six to eight tablespoonfuls good, New Orleans molasses, one pint of milk. Mix together very thoroughly. Put in muffin rings and bake in oven. About one ounce should be put in each ring as they raise easily. Eat with plenty of good butter. They should be given to children before each meal, when they are hungry, not after their stomachs are full. Put bran in dish first. Sift in flour, soda and salt. Mix these thoroughly together, then add one pint of milk (two cupfuls) and six to eight tablespoonfuls of New Orleans molasses. The quantity of molasses depends upon the individual taste. They are good for any child or adult whether constipation exists or not.

Drugs may be of temporary service in some cases. A pill of cascara sagrada is the best for this purpose. It should not be continued for more than two weeks. Castor oil, calomel, and other frequently-used cathartics should never be used in simple constipation.

TREATMENT OF OBSTINATE CONSTIPATION

There are cases that resist treatment of the kind described above. Diet and drugs do not succeed in establishing[Pg 312] the habit of daily bowel movements. In these cases radical treatment is imperative. The diet should be the same as that described above, but it will be found advisable to cut out milk altogether. Cereals can be taken with sugar and butter instead of milk. The oil injection plan of Professor Kerley has given me excellent results. I quote his comments upon and method of giving it:—

"Oil Injections."—"For this purpose a soft-bulb syringe of four ounces' capacity is ordered. Over the hard rubber tip is place a small sized adult rectal tube or a No. 18 American catheter. The catheter or tube is cut so that but nine inches remain for use. The cut end is forced over the small, hard rubber tip of the syringe. A fountain syringe is impracticable for this purpose, as it is soon destroyed by the oil and rendered unfit for use. Besides, sufficient pressure is not produced to force the oil into the gut even with a high elevation of the bag. The child is placed on his back or on his left side. The syringe is filled with oil, the tube is lubricated, and passed through the rectum as far as it can go. When it has been passed to the full nine inches, as may readily be done with a little practice, the syringe is emptied and the tube withdrawn. The injection should be given after the child has been placed in bed for the night. It is our object to have the oil retained during the night. If a passage of the bowels is produced at the time, or if the oil leaks out during the night, a small quantity should be used. In some of my patients I have been able to use but one ounce. In very few, indeed, does it cause an evacuation at the time. If there is a tendency to leakage a napkin should be worn to avoid soiling the bed-linen. The following morning after breakfast, the child is placed on the vessel and kept there until a bowel movement results or until fifteen minutes have elapsed. In a great many cases if the constipation has been obstinate for months, the bowel will be at once evacuated. When this does not occur in fifteen minutes, a glycerine suppository is inserted, which invariably produces an evacuation. This use of the suppository, according to my observation,[Pg 313] can usually be dispensed with in a very few days; the use of the oil, however, may have to be continued for several weeks. When the child has had the oil nightly and an evacuation the next morning without assistance for two weeks, I direct that the oil be omitted for a night and the effect noted. If the usual passage occurs after breakfast, the oil is given for five nights and then omitted. If the case progresses satisfactorily the use of the oil is gradually omitted, being given at first every second night, then every third, fourth, or fifth night, etc. A considerable number of cases have been completely relieved in two months. In the event of no passage following the omission of the oil, its use is continued for two weeks longer, when it is again omitted for a night." To illustrate this point the following case is cited.

"Illustrative Case.—A boy three years of age had never had a bowel evacuation without drugs, soap enemas, or suppositories since birth, and finally these were no longer effective. The mother, thoroughly frightened, brought the child to me. Eight months of diet and the use of the oil were required before he was entirely well. It is now three months since the local treatment was discontinued and the bowel function remains normal.

"The diet with the absence of milk must be continued for months after the patient is apparently well, and he must not be allowed to pass a single morning without an evacuation at the usual time. In assuming the management of one of these cases I explain to the mother or nurse that the treatment is not pleasant for the child or the attendant, and that it may have to be persisted in for weeks, and unless she is willing to carry it out to the end, it would better not be undertaken. I assure her, however, that with her coöperation, which is usually readily given, the child will make a complete recovery. Cases that are slow in responding to treatment, I usually give the additional advantage of abdominal massage from twenty minutes to one-half hour, before the child is placed at stool. The massage should practiced by one skilled in the work.

"The above local measures apply particularly to children[Pg 314] after the eighteenth month. They may be used earlier, however, following out the diet along the lines laid down for bottle-fed children who suffer from constipation. In very young children a smaller amount of oil should be used, never more than two ounces, usually one ounce is all that is required. When the oil treatment is under way, whatever the age of the patient, laxative drugs should not be given."

[Pg 315]

CHAPTER XXIII

CONSTIPATION IN WOMEN

Chief Cause of Constipation in Women—Constipation a Cause of Domestic Unhappiness—The Requirements of Good Health—The Cost of Constipation—Constipation and Social Exigencies—One of the Important Duties of Mothers—Constipation and Diseases of Women—Constipation is Always Harmful—Constipation and Pregnancy—Explanation of Incomplete Constipation—Causes of Constipation—Negligence—Lack of Exercise—Lack of Water—Lack of Bulk in the Food Taken—Abuse of Cathartic Drugs and Aperient Waters—Overeating—Treatment of Constipation in Women.

It has been stated that constipation is almost universal among the women of America. It is a fact that very few American women enjoy, to a reasonable degree, a permanently satisfactory bowel condition. Constipation is an acquired habit and unquestionably negligence is the primary and the chief cause of it. The negligence, no doubt, begins at a very early age; it is at least an established habit before any intelligent, consecutive effort is made to remedy it. Inasmuch as women are the mothers of the race, and as their part in the scheme of life *is* the supreme one; and as constipation has been shown to be a serious, far-reaching, significant disease, a very sincere and persistent crusade should be made to educate women as to its importance. For a less altruistic purpose, tremendous popular movements have been carried to success. For a less service rendered to the race names have achieved renown. In addition to the symptoms stated in the preceding paper, the condition which we now desire to emphasize is the effect of the constant self-poisoning on the general health and its effect upon a woman's reproductive efficiency.

The poison being constantly absorbed, means general bad health, bad health to a degree depending upon the degree of constipation which is the cause of the poisoning. It may be simply that the woman does not wholly enjoy good health, or that she is completely incapacitated[Pg 316] because of chronic bad health, or any degree of indifferent health between these two extremes.

If the degree of poison is sufficient to cause habitual poor health, its effect upon the blood must be bad, and the effect of the bad blood upon the nervous system and the other vital organs cannot be good. Now if this process has been going on for many years, the condition of the woman, who is its victim, as an efficient machine, compared with the woman in whom this condition never did exist, must be very different indeed. This condition of affairs—inasmuch as constipation is so common in women— must have a tremendous significance when estimating the vitality and efficiency of the coming generation.

We might go much further and yet be sure of our position, and maintain that it is this national autotoxemia, this scourge of womanhood, that is to a great extent responsible for the characteristic American "vice of neurasthenia," and of the domestic infelicity and unhappiness which are so common in the large cities of this country. If we add to the intestinal autotoxemia of constipation, the tendency to, or vice of, indiscriminate eating and drinking—of which the American people are particularly guilty—we would be on firmer ground. In fact we would feel that we had pointed out the one underlying cause of most of the domestic irritability prevalent to-day, which is of serious importance, and which is, fortunately, capable of correction. It is a matter of everlasting and continuous education.

The Requirements of Good Health.—There are certain fundamental basic requirements which are essential to good health: fresh air, good water, a reasonable amount of physical and mental exercise, nutritious food, freedom from unnecessary and unreasonable worry, frequent bathing, and a daily movement of the bowels. The reason why constipation is of such serious importance is because it is the only basic requirement of good health that afflicts a large majority of the race at the same time. The health of so many is being undermined by this one affliction, that it dominates all other factors that have any bearing upon posterity. A woman may enjoy all[Pg 317] the essential conditions necessary to good health, yet she may be constipated, and the presence of this condition will undermine, in her constitution, all the benefits she derives from her advantageous environments. It will do more; it will be responsible for the disposition,—the temperament,—of that woman. The natural disposition of that woman may be an amicable one; if it were allowed to express itself naturally it would be kind, gentle, considerate, affectionate. No woman, however, the victim of chronic constipation, can preserve an equable temperament or an amicable disposition. It is impossible—with her nerves being constantly poisoned—that she can hold the symptoms of that condition in abeyance. She must be irritable and nervous and sick of herself and everything and everybody. The home as a direct result suffers; its atmosphere is not one of contentment and peace and affection. Constipation, therefore, blights the home and the influence of one blighted home may have a far-reaching effect on the story of the human race. It is responsible also for that woman's mental attitude outside the home. Instead of exerting an optimistic influence, her whole existence is a message of pessimism and discouragement. Multiply these influences and messages to correspond with the prevalence of the disease and we have a condition that is tremendously significant, a condition that is really a pressing economic issue. A constipated woman is an anti-eugenist—a eugenic atrocity.

We have no desire to create a false impression or to build up a foolish fear. Are we justified in regarding this as one of the most important, if not the most important, disease condition; the most menacing physical vice, which the human race has to combat? Let us offer the following brief facts in witness of our stand:

The Cost of Constipation.—It has been estimated that consumption (the great white plague) kills one-tenth of all the human race. Cancer kills half as many, or one in every twenty. Constipation, and the diseases which are caused directly by it, kills one in every three of all the people on the civilized globe.

Constipation has been responsible for the expenditure[Pg 318] of millions of dollars in advertising in the newspapers alone,—more, probably, than has been spent in advertising remedies for all other diseases combined. Do you suppose this money was a donation? Do you suppose these keen, alert interpreters of the spirit of the times, the up-to-date business men, were not and are not aware that constipation is the "universal disease"?

Every drug store, in every civilized spot on earth, has its shelves loaded down with constipation remedies; dinner pills, liver pills, cathartic pills, tablets in all possible coatings and combinations, mineral waters from a multitude of springs, aperient drinks by the dozen, laxative teas and cordials, cathartic oils and emulsions. If the demand for these articles should cease most of the drug stores would close up.

Many millions of dollars have been made and are being made by various men and concerns, who have devised ingenious mechanical agencies which are supposed to cure, and in curing renew the lost health caused by constipation. We have in mind in this connection, a man who conceived the ingenious plan of putting the opening of an ordinary fountain syringe in the middle instead of at the end and made a fortune out of it. In this opening he places an upright nozzle, and instead of hanging the bag up and allowing the water to run into the bowel, he has the patient sit on the bag and thereby the water is forced into the bowel. He has written a two-hundred page book on the advantages of this idea, and his "literature" contains the names of famous men and women in all walks of life who use his device. The name of one of the famous judges of the Supreme Court of the United States was there; another was the name of a popular operatic beauty who writes for the daily press little essays on "How to be beautiful!" and "How to keep well!" He deserves his success. He is an emancipator and has doubtless done a great deal of good. His success demonstrates, beyond contradiction, the prevalence of the malady under discussion, and it must be remembered that he is only one of hundreds who garner from the same ample harvest.[Pg 319]

If we could estimate in value the economic loss sustained by the race because of the inefficiency of the victims of intestinal intoxication, due to constipation, the sum would be colossal. Even then it would only represent the direct economic deficiency—it would not express, nor could any figure adequately represent, the indirect loss sustained by the race because of the temperamental characteristics, which are the products of intestinal poisoning, and which produce domestic tragedies and economic failures.

Has this array of evidence any meaning, or does it just happen to be so? We leave it to the reader; if it stimulates thought, or pricks a conscience it will have done its duty.

Constipation and Social Exigencies.—The cause of constipation in women, whose social station commands every sanitary, hygienic, and dietary luxury, is their method of living, the food they eat, and the negligence which is almost obligatory because of social exactions. If constipation did not so frequently accompany "good" living (which is the modern name for overeating and drinking) we would have thousands and thousands of healthy, robust, contented women, fit and willing to assume the onerous duties concomitant with motherhood. All their enthusiasm, however, is expended in the effort to keep "in the ring," to overcome the effects of the poison of constipation, to preserve their youth and freshness, to undo what neglect has accomplished. It is because of the failure of this simple function that my lady seeks the masseur, the facial artist, the society doctor, the beauty expert, and the thousand and one agencies, which an extravagant and profligate age has made necessary to foster the efficiency of its votaries.

I am optimistic, however, regarding the future. I believe the human race is improving, despite the disadvantageous surroundings and conditions which hamper honest effort and stultify truth. A higher efficiency is the goal, and the intention is to obtain this desideratum by fair and by just means. There is an awakening, an unrest, a groping for knowledge in almost every field of human endeavor, and there is none in which the yearning[Pg 320] for fact, for truth, for instruction, is stronger and keener, than in the world-wide movement in the interest of a better motherhood, and in a more serious study of child life. It is an encouraging sign, a hopeful promise, of what the future has in store.

One of the Important Duties of Mothers.—The immediate lesson to be learnt from the facts just recounted is to instruct mothers in their duty toward their daughters. If each mother would retain the confidence of her daughter sufficient to instruct her in the duties which are important, how much needless suffering would be saved. To know as a matter of fact whether the daughter's bowels are in good condition will appeal to all who read this as being of very great importance. It is not only necessary to know if they have a movement every day, it is necessary to know the character of the daily movement; whether it is hard and dry and necessitates straining,—the evil consequences of which, in young girls, is very serious indeed,— or if it is habitually loose and suggestive of what has been described as incomplete constipation.

If the mothers of America would consecrate themselves to this simple task, who could tell in mere words the effect it would have on the race yet unborn? There are problems of scientific intent, and of fancy names, that engage the attention of philanthropically inclined ladies, and which are emblazoned on the society columns of the daily press, of much less importance to the human family than the homely duty we ask mothers to devote themselves to.

Constipation and Diseases of Women.—Constipation is present in a very large majority of the cases of diseases of women. It may be caused by disease of the womb, or it may cause disease of the womb. There is no question about the bad effect constipation has upon all diseases of this type. In many cases it is absolutely impossible to effect a cure without first curing the accompanying constipation.

We seldom appreciate how severe a degree of constipation a growing girl will submit to without seeking relief. Some of the worst cases of constipation that have been[Pg 321] known, have been in girls between the ages of sixteen and twenty. The mechanical effects of such a condition can well be imagined. The constant, severe straining, necessary to evacuate the bowel, has, in very many instances, produced congestion and displacement of the womb and ovaries. It is not observed at this time, or if observed it is not understood, and thus is laid the foundation for years of neurasthenia, helplessness, and disease.

The more we investigate the ramifications of constipation the more we learn of its seriousness and of its significance.

Constipation is Always Harmful.—There is no period in life when constipation can be borne with impunity. Youth, with its virility and vitality, will endure its consequences with an apparent negation, so far as positive or specific results are concerned, but it is only an apparent impunity. There is always a certain amount of strength built up, held in reserve as a heritage of youth, which will withstand a certain amount of physical license, but if this reserve is assailed by an unnecessary imposition, and is successfully undermined, there will be infinitely less reserve to call upon in the legitimate battle of life. Life is too real, too concentrated, too strenuous, and health is too precious to be wilfully wasted in any form of self-abuse.

Constipation and Pregnancy.—Mothers will appreciate from the foregoing explanation why constipation is eugenically a crime during pregnancy. The evils which result from constipation mechanically, frequently have serious consequences by interfering with the circulation of the blood to the womb, by forcing the womb to assume wrong positions, by straining at stool, and by preventing the kidneys from functionating properly; these may render the life of the pregnant woman miserable, and may be the direct cause of a painful, prolonged, difficult labor. The evils which result from constipation because of the absorption of poisons by the bowel are of the gravest importance during pregnancy. These poisons affect the general health; the victim is tired, listless, and apathetic, and is thereby disinclined to exercise adequately;[Pg 322] the appetite is poor; there are headaches, neuralgias, insomnia, nervousness, melancholia, and general mental and physical inertness. What hope may a pregnant woman entertain of having "an easy confinement," or of bringing a healthy child into the world under these circumstances? Who is to blame? Sometimes it is necessary to tell the unadorned truth,—the woman is to blame. No woman has a right to assume the responsibilities of maternity who has not had enough respect for herself to discontinue habits which caused this failing, or who has not had strength of will enough to begin its successful cure. Get busy,—do something,—it is never "too late," but do it now.

Before we take up the treatment of constipation in women, it is necessary to explain more fully the type of constipation which we referred to as "incomplete" constipation. There is a condition of the bowel, in which we find its wall coated with hard fecal matter. The size of the bowel may be dilated as a consequence. This condition may occupy part, or most, of the entire length of the large intestine. In the middle of this hard mass there is a small channel through which semi-liquid matter passes. When the bowel moves, it is this semi-liquid matter that passes out, and this constitutes the daily movement. We have consequently a condition in which we have a daily movement but not a complete emptying of the bowel. The character of the stools from such a bowel must necessarily be more or less of a semi-liquid consistency, because the intestine, being coated with a hard dried out layer of old fecal substance, is prevented from absorbing the liquid part of the fresh fecal mass passing through it. This condition may exist for a considerable time, but it will slowly undermine the health and vitality of any person in whom it exists. The symptoms which a patient in this condition complains of are,—a feeling of being tired and languid, no energy or vim, headache, loss of appetite, loss of flesh, neuralgic pains, nausea, vertigo (dizziness), insomnia, frequent colds, cold hands and feet, biliousness, sallow skin and muddy complexion, liver spots, coated tongue and a "bad breath," nervousness, melancholia, various abnormal conditions[Pg 323] and diseases of the skin, pimples, blackheads, eruptions, eczema, piles, appendicitis, diseases of the intestinal wall as a result of the constipation, Bright's disease of the kidney, and many other morbid conditions. Any physician could name many symptoms, which were never properly understood but which are now known to be caused by the absorption of poisons resulting from inactivity of the bowels. Patients may not necessarily have all of the above symptoms; they may have a number of them, or they may have all of them, and they may have others not mentioned at all.

Treatment of Constipation in Women.—To effect a movement of the bowels in a patient who is a victim of constipation is not a cure. We can indefinitely cause bowel action by drugs, etc., but the condition will remain the same or worse. When habitual constipation exists there is an underlying condition affecting the entire system which indicates that something is radically wrong. It may be necessary to change the whole routine of the patient's life. It will certainly be necessary at the very beginning to inquire into the daily diet, exercise, and surroundings.

During the past ten years there has been born every few days a new medical "ism," a new religious cult. Why? Because human nature is an unstable equation. We are never satisfied with the old order of things and there will always be a following wherever there is a leader. These "isms" and cults do not survive. Some seem to thrive, others die a natural death. There is a law, as old as the hills, that you cannot get something for nothing in this world. We learn its bitter truth as the years pass, and when we get over the day dreams and the sentiment of youth we settle down to real work. If we desire to retain good health, or regain lost health, we must do something. No one can hand it to us on a silver plate, nor can anyone work a miracle in our behalf. We cannot buy health, we must deserve it.

This is the secret of the success of all schemes to cure disease. The human family will not knuckle down and swallow the truth. The man or woman in poor health is looking for Aladdin's lamp everywhere and always. A[Pg 324] new bait, dressed up in lubricated, oily words, promising impossible results, will be accepted as the simple unadorned truth, and will be bought and paid for, in the end forgotten. The royal road, the easy road, which they are looking for is impossible. There is no way by which any one of us may continue to break the laws of nature and retain or regain our lost health. Miracles are impossible. Prayers without deeds are empty mouthings and a waste of time. Let us see how this works out in the treatment of constipation.

We must find the cause of the constipation. I will name the causes in their order of frequency.

Negligence.—This is unquestionably the primary cause of almost all cases of bowel inactivity. As has been already noted, the exigencies of modern life are of such a strenuous nature that we do not find the time to devote to this function the degree of systematic attention which it demands in order to preserve a healthy condition of intestinal regularity. The bowel is simply a complex muscle controlled by an elaborate system of nerves of an involuntary type. In order to preserve the highest degree of efficiency of this complicated mechanism, it must be permitted to obey the laws nature endowed it with and which it must obey. When the fecal mass reaches the rectum the nerve centers, acting through the spinal cord, send a message to the rectum something like this: "Empty yourself of your contents, we have made all preparations and everything is ready." The rectum obeys to the extent of notifying you that it wants to be relieved; you feel the desire to evacuate the bowels. If you obey, all is well, nature is appeased, you encourage the systematic regularity necessary to good health. If you do not obey, you upset the delicate mechanism, and frequent negligence of this character will result in the complete disarrangement of this complex machinery so that it will fail to warn you that a bowel movement is necessary and constipation is established. We must therefore retrace our steps and re-educate the bowel systematically to empty itself at a certain time every day. This can be done in nearly every case without artificial assistance. It may take time but it is worth[Pg 325] a little methodical persistence. The point is, you must do it; no "ism" or esoteric agency can do it for you.

Mothers will recognize from this explanation the necessity of establishing the habit in children at the earliest possible moment.

Lack of Exercise.—What does the word exercise imply? It implies movement, better circulation of the blood, better health and tone to every part of the body, more oxygen, and a richer, better quality of blood, and because of a better quality of blood, which is the fuel of the body machine, we have a better, smoother working machine. Every human being requires a certain amount of exercise; otherwise the machine will not run smoothly. If this exercise is not obtained, things begin to go wrong. One of the very first signs to indicate that the machine is not running as it ought to run, is a sluggish condition of the whole digestive apparatus and a certain degree of bowel inactivity (constipation) follows. There is no substitute for this need. Drugs will not help you, mechanical devices will not do the work for you, though they may aid you. You must do the work yourself. If you fail or hesitate to recognize the truth, if you temporize or procrastinate, you are only deferring the issue. The argument that you have not the time, that your work will not permit you, is no argument at all. You must do it or reap the consequences; you certainly cannot escape them. The wise woman accepts the situation, the fool goes to an early grave.

Lack of Water.—Constipation may be due to a deficiency of water in the system. Women who suffer from this type do not drink enough water. The bowel may be willing and able to do its duty, but is handicapped because a certain amount of liquid is essential to proper digestion and natural bowel activity. At least six glasses of water should be taken by every healthy adult human being in each twenty-four hours. The best time to take this water is as follows: one glass on arising, two between breakfast and lunch, two between lunch and dinner, and one on retiring. Between meals means one hour after a meal and at least one-half hour before the following meal. No liquid should be taken during a meal, or[Pg 326] immediately after, or before a meal. All water taken may be hot or cold, according to the fancy of the taker. It is of advantage to squeeze the juice of half a lemon into the water taken on arising if there is any tendency to constipation or if the liver is lazy or torpid. It is also good for the complexion.

Lack of Bulk in the Food Taken.—Sometimes the character of the food taken is such that there is no body to it. The process of digestion so completely liquefies it that the bowel has no solid matter to manipulate. To excite the peculiar movements of the intestinal wall there must be substance in the contents. The variety of the daily food must be so arranged as to provide this. A list of these foods is provided elsewhere in this book. Certain other foods stimulate intestinal activity, not because of their bulk, but because of the chemical elements they contain. All forms of sugar, the sugars of fruits, the acids of fruits and vegetables, are excellent natural laxatives. Sour milk and buttermilk, oils and fats, are also of distinct value in this respect.

On the other hand, soups, gruels, porridges, and purées are constipating because the digestive process reduces them to liquids and leaves no bulk for the bowel to act upon. New bread, hot biscuits, "noodles," and doughy foods are also objectionable, especially to children. Hot baths, hot drinks, hot enemas, and sweating are also constipating because they extract so much liquid from the bowel leaving the contents excessively dry.

Abuse of Cathartic Drugs and Aperient Waters.—This is a widespread evil; it may justly be regarded as a national curse. The victims of this custom do not realize that they are addicted to a habit which must be rightly regarded as equally as bad as the drink habit, so far as its ultimate effect on the general health and the prospect of longevity is concerned. Its popularity is a product of our national vice of indiscriminate eating and drinking. It is more common among the class who live in restaurants, hotels, and boarding houses, who keep late hours, eat late suppers and who do not exercise enough. These individuals eat too much and live too high. After a time the liver becomes sluggish, the stomach fails to[Pg 327] digest properly, the bowels lose their tone, and flatulent indigestion or some other more or less serious condition follows; to maintain the pace, to feel and keep fit, they discover that a glass of some advertised aperient or laxative water before breakfast works wonders, tides them over for the time being and keeps them "in the ring." They compliment themselves and push the specter of age aside.

The thought that they were not "as young as they once were," or that they must go slow, was not a very pleasing suggestion, so having found a "cure" by adding another bad habit on top of an existence which is composed of nothing but bad habits, they start all over again. The suggestion that their trouble is a warning that "things are going wrong" and that the whole plan of living must be radically and promptly changed does not meet with their approval, and so the Department of Health statistics heap up the records of deaths due to heart disease, hardening of the arteries, Bright's disease of the kidneys and apoplexy. It is not a happy tale, but the truth is often tragic.

When a woman finds that her physical efficiency depends upon the habitual use of cathartic drugs or laxative waters, she must regard the knowledge with respect, she must give it serious consideration, and she must adopt means to so change her method of living, that nature will be given a chance to work in her interest—not against her. Better to find out exactly where the trouble *is* now, and go after it than to travel too far along the wrong road. Many die from the "disease" of procrastination.

Overeating.—Overeating may be included in this classification because it so overworks the digestive apparatus that it is impossible for it satisfactorily to complete its function. Any reader desirous of understanding the full significance of overeating in this connection should carefully read the article on this subject on pages 289 and 290.

There are, of course, a great many other causes for constipation but these are the important ones. When we find the cause of any particular case it will suggest the remedy and we must employ it faithfully if we hope to[Pg 328] effect a cure. If it is negligence, we must correct that fault and compel our daily routine to accommodate itself to a regular observance of this function. If it is lack of exercise, we must get more exercise, or if it is lack of bulk in our food, we must change our method of living and select with more care the foods we eat. If it is lack of water, we can correct the constipation by adding the proper amount of water at the proper time.

A patient who has been a victim of chronic constipation for some time must live a life somewhat after the following general plan:

She should increase the vegetables, fruits, and fats in her diet and she should drink enough water. It is a good plan to sip slowly one-half pint of hot or cold water morning and evening. Daily exercise in the open air is advisable; exercise of some kind, even if taken indoors, is imperative. Walking, riding, bicycling, tennis, golf, swimming, are the best forms of exercise for women. Indoor gymnastics can be made a satisfactory substitute. After the exercise a hot shower bath and a cold sponge bath or cold plunge or a swim should follow.

Women in very moderate circumstances may walk briskly a distance of three or four miles, and on returning can take a warm bath followed by a brisk rub-off with a coarse towel wrung out of cold water, or they can use a hose with a spray nozzle and allow the cold water to run over them for a few seconds after the warm dip in the bath tub. After the adoption of these measures the bowels may tend to regulate themselves. If so, this is the proper time to cultivate the habit of regularity, by selecting a certain time each morning or before retiring for this function. The patient should go to the toilet at the regular time even if the desire is not present. By straining slightly, and by encouraging the voluntary desire, the bowel may receive the necessary stimulation and an evacuation may result. If there should seem to be no disposition on the part of the bowel to become accustomed to this procedure, we must aid it for the time being. A glycerine or soap suppository, a glass of aperient water, Pluto, Hunyadi, Apenta, or the imported Carlsbad salt in warm water, or the effervescent Citrate of Magnesium,[Pg 329] will result in a prompt emptying of the bowel. There are a great many other cathartic drugs and many well-known laxative pills, etc., but these are not necessary if a systematic effort is being made to cure the constipation, because success will come within a reasonable time if the patient will not become unduly discouraged. Many victims are deficient in fat; the bowel needs lubrication; we therefore recommend a good quality of olive oil, one tablespoonful after each meal. Frequently it is of advantage to inject, high up in the bowel, two or three ounces of sweet oil at night, as is done in children, and which is fully described in the previous chapter.

If the constipation is due to deranged nerves, in which the reflexes of the intestinal wall seem to share, we advise massage of the abdomen, and an occasional hot or cold rectal injection. The proper quantity to use for this purpose is from two to three quarts. The solution to use is the normal salt solution. See page 627.

In that form of incomplete constipation in which we stated that there was a layer of hard, impacted feces covering the bowel wall, a special method of treatment is necessary. In these cases nothing will succeed as satisfactorily as very hot, high rectal injections. The object of course is to rid the bowel of the old, hard, dry mass, which has collected there, before we can hope to get the bowel into condition to perform its own work. It is almost incredible that the human bowel can hold so much old dried-out, nasty stuff as is stored up in these constipated bowels. Hot salt water, as hot as can be tolerated, two or three quarts at a time, is the correct way to dislodge this mass. It will not be done at once; it frequently takes two or three weeks before the bowel is fairly clean. The irrigations should be given every second night until the bowel is clean. The method of giving these washings is fully described on page 312. While these irrigations are being given the patient should take olive oil by the mouth, one tablespoonful after each meal. The proper food, open-air exercise, sanitary living, plenty of water, and regular attention to the bowel movements will in the end cure the affliction.

www.ingramcontent.com/pod-product-compliance
Lightning Source LLC
Chambersburg PA
CBHW051833090426
42736CB00011B/1791